THE HOLY PLACE

THE
HOLY PLACE

*Decoding the Mystery
of Rennes-le-Château*

HENRY LINCOLN

ARRIS BOOKS
An imprint of Arris Publishing Ltd
GLOUCESTERSHIRE

For my children
Hugo, Caroline, Rupert and Kate,
to augment their childhood memories of
Rennes-le-Château.

For my grandchildren
who have yet to visit the place.

And especially for

J

who would dearly love to visit
somewhere else!

PRINTING HISTORY

First published in Great Britain by Jonathan Cape 1991
Corgi paperback edition published 1992
Reprinted paperback edition published by ARRIS BOOKS 2005
An imprint of Arris Publishing Ltd
12 Adlestrop, Moreton in Marsh, Gloucestershire GL56 0YN
www.arrisbooks.com

ISBN 1-84437-062-3

Printed and bound in Great Britain by Biddles Ltd, King's Lynn, Norfolk

Contents

Preface

All my life I had envied Howard Carter his glorious moment when he broke through into the Tomb of King Tutankhamen. Lord Carnarvon asked him: 'Can you see anything?' – and Carter, his eyes dazzled by that first glimpse of treasure, replied: 'Yes . . . wonderful things!'

I no longer envy that incredible discovery. In my turn I have caught sight of unexpected wonders, and more remain to be found. I have entered a 'treasure chamber' and begun to see what lies within. But I suspect that I have glimpsed only a small part of the treasure. In this book I hope to open a door to enable readers to make fresh discoveries for themselves. To experience, as I have done, that overwhelming shock of excitement at knowing that one's eyes are the first to see a long-lost marvel.

I have taken the first few steps along a new-old road. I cannot yet see where this road may lead, but already I know that we have much still to learn about the thinking and capabilities of our remote ancestors. This book is a sign-post along the way back to a lost understanding. The journey thus far has been long and not without detours and stumbling blocks. It was not a journey I had intended to make.

H.L.

Preface to the 2005 edition

This book was first published in 1991 – this introduction to the new edition, to be published in 2005, demands both apology and explanation. It had been my intention to prepare an entirely new version – with the diagrams superimposed upon the map – and with perhaps, both foreword and postscript, in order to bring the book 'up-to-date.' Life and Time, however, have dictated otherwise.

First then, my apology. The book is reprinted – this preface apart – as an <u>exact</u> reprint of the original. As my publishers have pointed out, there is now a new generation of readers who are unfamiliar with this title – the only one of my books to have disappeared from the bookshop shelves – and who have been waiting too long for me to snatch the time to do the necessary work. But what of my explanation?

A great number of new readers have been attracted to the Mystery of Rennes-le-Château by the recent appearance of a fictional thriller – *The Da Vinci Code*. Jolly a read this may be . . . but it bears only a very slight resemblance to the truth of the story. Unfortunately, the author of the thriller has convinced many people of the 'reality' of much of what is highly questionable. For those who wish to acquaint themselves with the real background, I can do no better than refer them to my *Key to the Sacred Pattern*, first published in 1997.

This present little volume is necessary reading for newcomers who are looking for 'the truth' behind the myth. Nowhere else have I spelled out the mechanics of the ciphers . . . the first tentative steps into the geometric mystery . . . the first attempts to understand.

More than once, I have been asked if I 'still stand by' what I have written in my earlier books. The answer to this question is – of course –

yes. For this reason the present reprint stands with its errors uncorrected. What, then, are these errors?

First – and naturally – there are the typographical errors to be found in any published work . . . but these should be minor. Second – and all-encompassing – is my use of language. I have, throughout *The Holy Place*, used such words as 'exact' and 'precise.' I do not apologise for their use, though I feel that a word of explanation is due to my readers. And not least, because there are those who delight in 'catching out' such writers as myself. *Of course*, I am aware that there is a 'scientific' sense in which these words can be used – and I can – and do – use them in this sense when occasion demands. It is *not*, however, the sense in which I employ them in this – nor in the majority of my other writing. I intend such words to convey the meaning attached to them by 'the averagely intelligent reader.' I leave them here because I consider that it would be dishonest to alter them, for no matter what reason.

The value, if any, of such a reprint as this, lies in its provision of an historical perspective . . . a glance back at the manner in which a body of research develops and changes with the passing of time. How could I possibly have possessed in 1974, the knowledge which I had acquired by 1994? Or 2004? *Of course*, my ideas have grown and changed with the years. How could it be any other? And so, as I look back, I can see things which I would change – were I to be writing this book in 2005. But I am not.

When I first found the geometry in the Rennes-le-Château landscape, I was stunned. I had no reason to expect the extent to which this amazing discovery was going to grow. I cheerfully employed such words as 'exact,' thinking that the wonder was enough if its exactitude was to within – let us say - ten yards. I can remember my BBC director, Roy Davies, saying: 'If you show me an intersection anywhere in the village, I'll be impressed.' Almost two decades later, we all know better.

H.L.
April 18th 2005

I

First Encounters

The most casual and mundane of actions can sometimes change the course of one's life. So it was for me in 1969 when idly I spun a pavement bookstand outside a papershop in a small provincial French town. I was looking for some light and entertaining reading, something undemanding to fill a holiday hour. I reached out and took from the rack *Le Trésor Maudit* ('The Accursed Treasure'). As I handed over the few francs for the paperback, I had no inkling that I had just purchased twenty years of excitement, mystery and discovery. As haphazardly as a roulette wheel the spinning bookstand had presented me with a winner.

The book proved ideal for my purpose. It was an intriguing buried treasure mystery. The story concerned a tiny village – Rennes-le-Château – set on a mountain top in the foothills of the Pyrenees. At the end of the nineteenth century, the parish priest had discovered some mysterious parchments in his church. They had, it seemed, changed the life of the priest from church-mouse poverty to Croesus riches. They had led him, the book suggested, to a lost, an 'accursed', treasure. The accursed element was somewhat vague. There had been a few apparently unexplained deaths of people associated (more or less) with the story. The treasure itself seemed equally elusive. The book could give no firm details of its nature, though the priest certainly seemed to have acquired sudden and immense wealth.

The tale appealed to my enquiring spirit. The story was not set in a remote and fairy-tale past, nor was it a novel whose details could be

9

The priest with his housekeeper in the garden of the villa Bethania built with his new-found wealth.

altered to suit the writer's whim. The book claimed to be dealing with solid, verifiable fact. The priest had discovered the parchments in 1891 and had survived to enjoy the fruits until his death in 1917. His housekeeper, who had lived with him since his arrival in the village in 1885, was said to have shared the priest's secret, and she had lived on until 1953. The story was firmly rooted in 'today', so the author could – and presumably did – glean most of his information from the firsthand accounts of witnesses who had known the major protagonists in his story. There were also the tangible remains of the priest's activities which seemed to confirm a dramatic increase in his re-sources. His account books had survived, recording the depth of the poverty from which he had risen. In 1885 his income had been so pitifully small that he had been compelled to rely on the generosity of his parishioners in order to survive. By the time of his death he had spent millions on building, high living, and charitable good works. Here was a classic 'hidden treasure' story.

A page from the priest's account books for the year in which he allegedly
discovered the parchments.

Lying in the shade of a chestnut tree, relaxed under the warm
summer sun, I finished the book. I considered my few francs well
spent. The paperback had entertained me, had told a good tale and had
put not too great a strain on my credulity. In a few days it would be
forgotten. On my lap the book had fallen open at the page which
reproduced one of the curious parchments found by the priest. There
was nothing at all exceptional in the text of the document. A few lines
from the Gospels in Latin: ET FACTUM EST EUM IN SABBATO SECUNDO
. . . 'And it came to pass on the second sabbath . . . ' My eyes began
to close in that comfortable holiday torpor that comes when work,
responsibilities, pressures are far away. The Latin text swam mean-
inglessly before me. Unthinking, it seemed randomly, I began to pick
letters off the page. A . . . D . . . A . . . G . . . Suddenly I jerked
upright. It was as if someone had clashed mighty brazen cymbals two
inches from my ear. I was spelling out a message. Not in Latin, but in
French! A DAGOBERT II ROI ET A SION EST CE TRESOR ET IL EST LA MORT.

Now indeed I had a mystery. I searched my memory, riffling through the pages of the book for confirmation. But, no – nowhere had the author mentioned this message. Why not? He had spoken of hidden messages. He had referred to King Dagobert II. But he had not spelled out what I had just found. THIS TREASURE BELONGS TO DAGOBERT II KING AND TO SION AND HE IS THERE DEAD.

Yet it was so simple to find – the kind of code-making game that children play. No one who set out to write a book about this subject could fail to examine the parchments with some attention. It followed that the author of the book must have found what I had found – and as easily as I had found it. Why then had he remained silent? It was exactly the titillating piece of evidence which would have helped to sell his book. His silence seemed senseless. Unless . . .

I decided to read the book again with more care. Perhaps there were other discoveries to be made. For a year or so the book was my constant companion. More entertaining than a crossword puzzle, the repro-duced parchments provided me with hours of absorbed fascination. Slowly faint glimpses of other layers of meaning began to emerge but they were merely tantalising fragments. Nothing was as clear, direct and meaningful as that first clangorous message. The simple school-boy code was there to serve a purpose, yet it was too easy to find for the information to be valuable. The message must be intended to attract attention. It was saying – 'Yes, there are secret messages here. Keep looking.' I kept looking. In the hunt for new ideas, new angles of approach, I began to research the background to the story.

Rennes-le-Château is in the Languedoc, a region of France which is both overwhelmingly beautiful and blessed with many traces of a rich and turbulent past. Here the Cathare heresy had taken root, flourished and been viciously suppressed by the Roman Church. In these mountains, the Knights Templar, proud warrior monks, had estab-lished castles and commanderies. Arab invaders, Visigothic hordes, crusading armies – all had passed this way. Behind the story of the nineteenth century priest and his tiny village lay long centuries of blood, fire, faith and suffering; fascinating and exciting glimpses of French history, little known and only sketchily taught here in Eng-land. As a writer for television, I could see that the material was ideal for a documentary film, especially with the added spice of the modern treasure hunt and my own deciphering of the 'secret' message.

The subject seemed right for the BBC's historical and archaeologi-cal series, 'Chronicle'. Paul Johnstone, 'Chronicle's' producer, agreed, and in December 1970 he sent me to Paris to talk to Gérard de Sède, the author of *Le Trésor Maudit*. Now, at last, I would be able to put the question which had baffled me at the very outset of my interest in the story. 'Why didn't you publish the hidden message?' Time and again I had tried to imagine what his reply might be. None of my guesses even approached de Sède's answer: 'Because we thought it might interest someone like you to find it for yourself.'

The identity of that mysterious 'we' and the true nature of de Sède's role as a front-man for others who remained in the shadows were to take years to unravel. But from that curious first meeting with de Sède I sensed that I was dealing with something more than a treasure-hunt story. In the decade that followed I made three films for the BBC, reporting the progress of my researches in *The Lost Treasure of Jerusalem . . . ?*, *The Priest, the Painter and the Devil* and *The Shadow of the Templars*. The films caught the imagination of an ever-growing and fascinated audience.

The complex and wide-ranging nature of the historical background had proved a fertile ground for new discoveries, new unexpected connections. These were developed in a book which I wrote with Michael Baigent and Richard Leigh. *The Holy Blood and the Holy Grail* was published in 1982 and became an immediate best-seller, and in 1986 we explored yet more ramifications of the mystery in *The Messianic Legacy*. These books will provide general historical background to the story of Rennes-le-Château but are not essential to a proper understanding of the astonishing account I am about to unfold here.

By the mid-80s Rennes-le-Château had spawned an industry. Other writers were bringing their own ideas, their own solutions to the mystery. Most of them, it must be said, veered towards wishful-thinking. Inevitably, solutions depended largely upon subjective interpretation of the evidence. Some were frankly dotty – as indeed were our books considered to be by the more blinkered or fiercely committed of Christians. Even so, Rennes-le-Château was now known around the world. The sleepy hamlet which I had first come to know in the early 70s was now on the tourist map.

After the publication of *The Messianic Legacy*, I considered that my work on the story was done. I could not see and certainly did not anticipate that I might have any further contribution to make to the ever-growing torrent of ink being poured upon the mystery. Yet Rennes-le-Château would not leave me alone. Since the outset of my researches I had been looking for the demonstrable and provable; for certainties which were solid, objective, unarguable. From the tranquillity of what I thought of as my retirement from the fray, I saw how few were the certainties on which the whole saga had been built. Even the basic facts, such as the story of the priest and his treasure, were essentially based upon hearsay evidence. From the priest's account books to the lists of Templar Grand Masters, from the Grail Romances to the story of the early church – too much was being taken as gospel. Even the Gospels themselves! How could one *know* that lists of Grand Masters were reliable? How could one know that the priest *had* found a treasure? How could one know that Jesus was born of a Virgin? Or that he had been born at all? In religion, acts of faith are inevitable. The Creed is a statement of belief, not of knowledge. I felt bound to ask myself: what did I KNOW about the story of Rennes-le-Château? And the answer to that question was: 'remarkably little'.

I decided to list the certainties. First, then, what did I know of the priest? I knew his name – it was Bérenger Saunière. I had seen it carved upon his tombstone. Beyond that . . . nothing. For every other scrap of knowledge concerning the man I had to rely upon what others had said. Did I *know* that he had found a treasure? No. I knew only that it has been reported that he found a treasure. Did I know that he had found the parchments? Again, no. Indeed, there are people who claim to know that the parchments are modern forgeries. In fact, such people 'know' no such thing; they know no more than I do – that two documents, supposedly copies of those found by the priest, existed and have been reproduced. Of their origins, nothing can be said with certainty. However, no matter what their provenance, the parchments certainly contain ciphered messages. Some of these messages I have found for myself and I have been given the key to the decipherment of others. One of these ciphers refers to the seventeenth century painter, Nicolas Poussin, and has led to the identification of a tomb near to Rennes-le-Château which, in its construction and mountain setting, is identical to the one depicted in the artist's most famous painting, *The Shepherds of Arcadia*. Here, too, was a certainty.

There was also the underlying geometric sub-structure of one of the parchments. This brilliant construction I shall demonstrate later in this book. Since 1971, when I first discovered it, this piece of evidence has remained one of the most impressive of my certainties. The geometry which I found was pentagonal – an irregular five-pointed star. When I later stumbled upon a complex hidden geometry in

Poussin's *The Shepherds of Arcadia*, this, too, was proved to be pentagonal in a superb analysis made by Professor Christopher Cornford of the Royal College of Art. Another certainty. Professor Cornford's work had made me turn my attention to the landscape of Rennes-le-Château and its surrounding area and this led to the discovery of the astonishing natural pentagon of mountains which I revealed in 1979 in my television film, *The Shadow of the Templars*.

Here then was my bedrock, the unassailable pieces of evidence which were demonstrable and provable. Everything else was a compound of hypothesis, or hearsay, or based upon documents which were open to falsification. As I contemplated my handful of certainties I realised that, without exception, they all led back to Rennes-le-Château – to the physical location of the village and its immediate environs. Years of historical research had served to build a dramatic backdrop to the mystery while leading further and further away from the place itself. It was as if Saunière and his treasure mystery had been acting as a fluttering banner set high on the ramparts of a castle. The mystery was attracting attention away from the solid structure upon which it was set. That structure of certainties which underlay all the research was reduced to Rennes-le-Château and its association with pentagonal geometry. This, in truth, was all I had. But it proved to be enough.

Within a week of turning my full attention to those few certainties I had glimpsed a new truth. Within three months the shape of an astonishing wonder had begun to emerge. Based upon certainty, itself a certainty, there was no need to hypothesise. Here was an objective discovery of staggering proportions – and it was unarguable.

Now, when I stand beside Saunière's grave, I feel the urge to reach down into the earth and shake those mouldering bones back to life. For twenty years he has led me a curious dance. I have chased many a false lead, leaped to many a deceptive conclusion, been blinded by ingenious smoke-screens, by clues strewn by him and others before him to conceal an astonishing fact. I cannot even be certain that Bérenger Saunière knew it, but his village has provided me with one more certainty. Rennes-le-Château is a small part of a greater wonder. The Eighth Wonder of the Ancient World.

2

The Mystery of Rennes-le-Château

'At the very mention of buried treasure all the dream and greed muscles begin to tense.' Thus a journalist accurately reflected the reaction to the first BBC film on Rennes-le-Château. The glint of gold is indeed a powerful attraction, though in this case it would be more accurate to call it a dis-traction. The complex background to the story of Rennes-le-Château has certainly merited investigation, but that background has equally certainly been the red herring which has delayed the discovery which is the subject of this book. All the necessary clues have long been available. In effect, the discovery has already been revealed – at least partially – though the distractions have been too powerful to make it evident. I now find it ludicrous to realise how I have paraded all the relevant indications in the three 'Chronicle' films without anyone noticing the glaringly obvious – myself included. Like Howard Carter, I had broken through into the 'treasure chamber', though it was almost twenty years before I noticed the 'wonderful things' that lay within. In company with the millions who watched those films, I looked without seeing.

The discovery which I have at last made establishes why Rennes-le-Château is surrounded by an aura of mystery. The place itself is a mystery. The enigma of the treasure and the parts played by Bérenger Saunière, the Knights Templar, the Cathares, are no more than mystification. The story of Rennes-le-Château may explain the events that have happened there, but those events are not relevant to the present book. In these pages I am not concerned with what has happened but with what exists – with the fact that this corner of Southern France is a temple, a Holy Place, which was constructed with enormous labour and skill in the remote past. Unlike other great works of early civilisation, this Temple has not fallen into ruin and decay. It is still as real and tangible as it was on the day of its completion – and yet, for all that, it is invisible. Not as the result of some arcane act of mumbo-jumbo magic. Not (as I know some would wish) because it is the fruit of some unknown super-race with mystic powers. The Temple is invisible simply because it is too vast to be seen. How visible is St Paul's Cathedral to an ant crawling across its floor? And it is on such a scale that the builders worked. The Temple of Rennes-le-Château is perhaps the largest structure ever built by man upon the face of the earth.

In order to grasp the significance of this colossal undertaking it must not be considered from a twentieth century viewpoint. The modern, sceptical, rationalist view of the universe was not shared by our remote forebears. To comprehend what they did at Rennes-le-Château – and why they did it – one must try to see the world, however faintly, through their eyes. To catch a glimpse of their awe and wonder. To sense, as they did, the power and presence of their gods. What our ancestors found here was enormously significant to them. Their gods had given them a Sacred Place, and so they built a stupendous Temple to enclose it.

The rediscovery of that Temple answers many questions – but it raises many others. How did the existence of such a wonder come to be forgotten? Why have those few who have learned of its existence remained silent when such a secret cries out to be revealed?

When the Barber of Midas learned that the king had the ears of an ass, he felt compelled to unburden himself of the amazing news. Unable to speak openly, he dug a hole in the ground and whispered his knowledge there. But the grasses grew and spoke his secret in the sighing of the wind. In just the same way, Poussin, Saunière and others through the years have felt the need to speak of the incredible secret of Rennes-le-Château. But they have also felt a mysterious constraint and so they have spoken in riddles. They have left us tantalising hints and clues, they have also laid false trails. As much effort seems to have been expended on attempts to conceal the truth as to reveal it.

In the pages which follow, I shall lead the reader through the labyrinth of clues which have led to the discovery of the Holy Place.

The extraordinary, painstaking and dedicated ingenuity which the clue-makers employed will amply demonstrate how important to them was the task which they had undertaken.

What follows is no light-hearted game.

*

The essential starting point for this investigation is Saunière's alleged discovery of two parchments in 1891.

ÉTFACTVMESTEVMIN
SAbbATOSECVNdΘPKIMO à
bIREPERSCCETESdIBGIPVLIAVTEMILLTRISCOE
PERVNTVELLERESPICASETFRICANTESMANTbVS + MANdV
CAbANTQVIdAMAVTEMdEFARISAEISAT
CEbANTELECCEQVIAFACIVNTdISCIPVLITVISAb
bATIS + QVOdNONLICETRESPONdENSAVTEMINS
SETXTTAdEOSNVMQVAMbOC
LECISTISQVOdFECITdAVTddVANdO
ESVRVTIPSEETQVICVMEOERAI + INTROIbITINdΘMVM
dEIETPANESPROPOSITIONIS   KEdIS
MANdVCAVITETdEdITETQVI   bIES
CVMERANTUXUB QVIbVSNO
NLICEbATMANdVCAHESINON   SOLIS SACERdOTIbVS

(P ⅃)

Parchment One

When a story bears the label 'Mystery' and is filled with enigmatic hints and clues, we expect the solution to be difficult. After all, if it were easy, there would be no mystery. We bring our sophistication to the problem and we hunt out the complexities. Sometimes we miss the obvious which is staring us in the face. Some of the clues are difficult to unravel – but some are not. Some of them will seem blindingly simple, when explained. Many people have spent much time in study of the documents here reproduced and have found little. Some have built solutions based upon no more than possibilities which are in themselves extremely flimsy and open to argument. As will be seen, when a correct solution is arrived at, there is no question of doubt. An accurate reading will include its own confirming proof.

JESVSCVRGOANTCCSCXATPESPASCShLCVENJTTbCTh9ANTAMVRAT
FVCRAOTIAZA•VVSMOKTYVVS9VCMMSVSCTYTAVITIYCSVSFCACCKVNT
LAVICM•TTCACNAPMTbTCTOMARThAhMINISTRRAbATCbLSLRVSO
VCROVNXVSCKATTC×ATSCOVMLCNTATLVSCVJMMARTALCKGOACbCCP
TTCKThRAMYNNGCNTTJNLKATPFTSTTCT9PRCTTOVSTCTVNCXTTPC
APCSTCKVLCTCXTCJRSTTCAYPTIKTSNSVJSPCPACSCKTPTCTAOMbCSTM
YLFTTLCSTCCXVNGCTNTTOALCKCATXALTCKGOVRNVMCXAGTSCTPVhL
TSCTVTXTVALXSCARJORTIS9VIYCKATCVhMTRAATTTVRYS9TVARChOCCVN
bCN VTVMNONXVCNVTTGRCCCNPATSACNLLKVSCTAALTVMCSGTC
GCNTCS? ATXTNVFCMhOCCNON9VSTALCGLCNTSPCKRTINCbCAT
LACVTMSCA9VhnFVKCLKTCTLOVCVIOSHCLhCNSCCA9VLCMVTTICbL
NMTVRPOTKAbCTCATXTTCJRGOTCShVSSTNCPTLLLMVNTTXATRMS
CPVLGTVKACMSCLCSCRVNCTILL9VAPLVPJCRCSCNhTMSCMPGCRhL
bCMTTSNObLTISCVMFMCLVTCTMNONSCSMPCRhLVbCTISCJOGNO
VILTCKOTZVRbAMV9LTLCXTMVALCTST9VTATLOLTCCSTXCTVCNC
LKVNTNONNPROTCPRTCSVMCTANTVM MSCAVTLVZLKVMPVTALK
Ch•T9VCM KSVSCTAOVTTAMORKTVTSCPOGTTAVKCRVNTAhVTCMP
KVTNCTPCJSSACCKCAOTVMVMTCTLAZCLKVMTNLTCKFTCTIRCNTY
LVTAMYLVTTPROP9TCKTLhXVMLbThGNTCXVGTALCTSNCTCKCA
ACbLNTTINTCSVM

NO₽IS

JÉSV. MCACLL .VVLNCKVM ✠ SPCS.VNL. PŒNITCNTIVM.
PCR.MAGALLNX. LACKYMAS ✠ PCCCATA. NOSTRA . ATLVAS.

Parchment Two

It must immediately be said that it matters not the slightest to this investigation if these clues are genuine (i.e. old) or fake (i.e. modern). Their reported history is confusing.

Saunière supposedly found the two parchments in a hollow pillar which supported the altar of his church. They came to light, it is said, when he undertook some necessary repair work. Other accounts imply that he found them because he was looking for them. Yet others insist that the documents were concocted in the recent past; that they contain nothing of interest.

Bérenger Saunière beside the pillar in which he supposedly found the parchments. Before he removed it to the church garden, where it still stands, the pillar had been a support for the altar.

In 1978, Pierre Plantard de St Clair (said then to be the Grand Master of the secret society of the Priory of Sion) informed me flatly that the parchments were cooked up in the 1950s by a man called Philippe de Chérisey, who was present when this statement was made. He would neither confirm nor deny it. Later M. Plantard qualified his statement. 'De Chérisey's confections', he said, 'were closely based upon very good originals'.

René Descadeillas, Curator of the Library of Carcassonne and a noted local historian, fiercely opposed to any investigation of Rennes-le-Château, told me categorically that there were no hidden messages in the documents. What I had found, he suggested, was the product of my own fevered imaginings. A similar problem of provenance applies to the tombstones of Marie de Négri D'Ablès, Dame d'Hautpoul de Blanchefort, which are strongly linked to the parchments.

This grave was supposedly in the cemetery at Rennes-le-Château and Saunière is said to have effaced the two inscriptions. Unknown to him, however, they had already been recorded in a book entitled *Pierres Gravées de Languedoc* by Eugène Stublein, and it is from this book that the published copies are alleged to have been taken. Curiously, no copy of this book has ever come to light. Some researchers have therefore rashly dismissed the grave inscriptions as modern fakes and worthless, intended merely to distract the gullible. Although it may be true that the Stublein book is a fiction, at least one of the inscriptions, that on the pointed headstone, was reproduced in a pamphlet entitled 'Excursion du 25 Juin 1905, à Rennes-le-Château' by E. Tisseyre, published by the Société d'Etudes Scientifiques de l'Aude in 1906. This pamphlet is unlikely to be a fake. But for all the necessary caution which must be brought to a study of these pieces, this investigation will prove a connection between the inscriptions and the two parchments, which will be seen as the work of the same hand. If genuine, that hand would seem to belong to the priest of Rennes-le-Château at the time of Marie de Blanchefort's death in 1781, the Abbé Antoine Bigou, but whether the creator of this material was Bigou or a modern

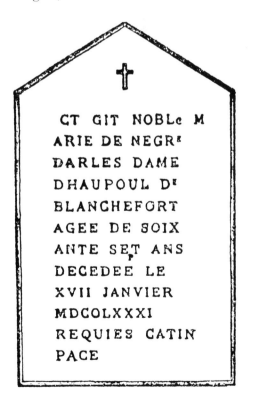

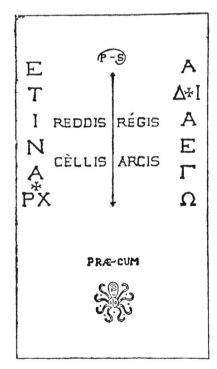

faker, he was undoubtedly a brilliant code-maker. No matter what might be one's opinion on the source of the material, the content remains unaffected, and it is with the content that we are here concerned. What, then, lies hidden beneath the innocent-seeming surface?

The fact that the written texts are in Latin and French deters many people who lack a knowledge of these languages from attempting any de-coding, but numerous indicators are clearly visible and should be readily identifiable, even if not immediately understood. For this reason, the reader is urged to attempt at least a few unguided steps through the labyrinth of clues, to devote at least the time that might be spent on a crossword puzzle in contemplation of the parchments and grave inscriptions. Such a brief preliminary study at this point will certainly serve to demonstrate something – if only that the obvious can easily be overlooked.

*

The cryptic messages are hidden with varying degrees of subtlety. First, there are the carrots – the simple codes which function only as encouragements to look further. The description which follows will be an attempt, where appropriate, to outline the thought processes which led to the various decipherments.

Parchment One is a clearly written Latin text. It will be immediately comprehensible to anyone with a knowledge of the language, such as a Catholic priest. Saunière would certainly have been able to read it. The text is a compound of the several different Gospel versions of the story which tells of Jesus and the disciples walking in the corn-fields on the Sabbath day – 'and they did rub the ears of corn and did eat.' Although the text is clear there is the instantly obvious oddity of the lines being arranged in a curious fashion, ending sometimes in the middle of a word when there would be ample space for its completion. (For example: 'coeperunt' – one word split between lines 3 and 4.)

Parchment Two is slightly, very slightly, less easily read than Parchment One, for a reason which will be explained below. For the moment it is only necessary to consider the superficial appearance, visible even without a knowledge of the Latin language. In contrast to the uneven line lengths of Parchment One, this is a more neatly laid out block of text. Neat, that is, except for the oddly untidy device in the bottom righthand corner.

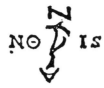

This could be interpreted as an ill-drawn arrow, a sort of direction indicator, especially as there is an N at the top which could denote North. The NO and IS seem without meaning, though there appears to be a more tidy arrowhead at the bottom of the device. A moment's attention to this arrowhead reveals it to be the letter A written upside-down. If the document is now inverted in order to turn this letter A upright, the NO – IS converts itself simply to SI ON which is, at least, meaningful. (Sion could mean Jerusalem, or it could be a reference to The Priory of Sion.) Returning to Parchment One, the confirmation of this key word is to be found in the apparently arbitrary variation of the line lengths. The four lines which form a block at the bottom left end with these same letters: S I O N.

Having found a helpful significance in the inverted A of Parchment Two, it is not too great a leap in the dark to consider a possible significance in the letter 'a' at the end of line 2 of Parchment One. This 'a' is easily identifiable as being the only letter which is isolated in the text and is part of the first deliberately broken word: 'abire'. A mere glance is sufficient to notice the further difference in the writing of this letter 'a' for it is clearly slightly higher on the line than are the adjacent letters. Laying a straight edge along the base of the letters in this second line of text reveals that there are two more raised letters: the fifth, which is another 'a', and the thirteenth, a letter 'd'. Continuing the hunt for raised letters, one finds the following:

In line   1 – there are none.

In line   2 – ð   d   ð

In line   3 – G   O

In line   4 – b

In line   5 – E   R   T

In line 6 – **| |**

In line 7 – **R O |**

In line 8 – **E T a**

In line 9 – **S | O N** (yet again)

In line 10 – **E S T C E TR**

In line 11 – **E S O R**

In line 12 – **ET | IES**

In line 13 – **T**

In line 14 – **L a M O R T**

Truly the simplest of boy-scout codes. The Latin text has yielded a French message which can now be read by taking the letters as they come in sequence:

A DAGOBERT II ROI ET A SION EST CE TRESOR ET IL EST LA MORT.

'This treasure belongs to Dagobert II King and to Sion and he is there dead.'

An alternative reading of IL EST LA MORT could be 'It is Death'. Though more dramatic, it is slightly the more questionable of the two renderings. There are no accents in the written text to give firmly 'là' (there) rather than 'la', the definite article for the noun 'la mort' (death). Nevertheless, for a more correct rendering of 'It is death', the French should read: 'C'est la mort'. 'It is death' is certainly more satisfying. It is vague enough to lead nowhere and it avoids the question: who is the 'he' that is there dead? Dagobert's remains are known to be elsewhere.

Be that as it may, so childishly hidden a message cannot be expected to yield on its own any greatly significant data. It is enough, though, to whet the appetite in the hunt for more tangible leads. It is also food for thought. Equally food for thought – perhaps indeed more so – is an explicit statement in the same parchment. In the bottom righthand corner two words have been separated from the body of the text: 'SOLIS SACERDOTIBUS'. Above them are two other words: 'REDIS BLES', which are not part of the biblical passage.

'Redis' could be a variant of one of the old names of Rennes-le-Château. The place took its name from the ancient Celtic Rhedones tribe and has been called (with many different spellings), Aereda, Redes, Rehennes, Rhedis and Reddis. 'Blés', however, is not a Latin word at all – enough to make it stand out as a signal to the decipherer. The word is French and means 'corn'. It is also used as a slang term for gold, money, treasure. (As 'bread' in modern Anglo-American parlance.) REDIS BLÉS SOLIS SACERDOTIBUS can therefore be interpreted to mean: 'The corn of Redis (is) only for the priesthood', i.e., The treasure of Rennes-le-Château is only for the initiated.

In Parchment Two there is yet another clearly visible 'hidden' text. Eight letters are much smaller than the rest of the writing. Taken in sequence they spell REX MUNDI – 'King of the World'. This is an epithet which was applied to the creative God of Evil by the Cathares, or Albigensians, a Christian sect which flourished in the Languedoc in the twelfth and thirteenth centuries. The Cathares were bloodily and ruthlessly suppressed as heretics by the Roman Church in the Albigensian Crusade which ended in 1244. The Cathares believed that all physical matter, the whole created universe, was the work of a God of Evil – Rex Mundi – who stood in opposition to the God of Good. Rex Mundi is therefore taken by some to be the Devil though, for the Cathares, he was not quite the Devil of conventional Christian theology and the term was, for them, equally applicable to the Pope.

But of what use is this in the hunt for secret messages? The hidden words 'Rex Mundi' must have a significance, if only as a red herring. In preparation for what is to follow, it should be pointed out that most complex ciphers require a key – a word or phrase which can be used to decipher the code. 'Sion' or 'Rex Mundi' would certainly be perfectly adequate for such a purpose. Inevitably the clues must be leading towards a more complicated cipher in which they may come into play.

There remains yet another and slightly more carefully hidden phrase which could also function as such a key. With an awareness of the earlier useful significance of the letter 'a', which helped to identify the 'Dagobert' message, a careful examination of Parchment Two reveals that this letter is always written thus: $\mathbf{a}$ – except in two cases.

In the tenth line of this text there is a clearly written **A** and in the eleventh line 'a' is written as **Ω**, Alpha and Omega – the first and last letters of the Greek alphabet and two letters of profound Christian significance – 'Christ is the Alpha and the Omega, the Beginning and the End.'

A brief digression here is necessary for the sake of those readers who have no knowledge of Latin and so will not have been able to study the actual text of the documents. Parchment Two is the 'Vulgate' Latin version of St John's Gospel, Chapter XII, verses 1–11. The passage concerns the visit of Jesus to the house of Lazarus in Bethany, when Mary Magdalene anointed His feet with oil and wiped them with her hair. As noted above, this text presents a slight difficulty to the reader, for a reason which will be immediately noticeable to anyone with a knowledge of Latin. Inserted into the body of the text are a large number of additional letters. For example, the first three words should read 'Jesus ergo ante'. As can be clearly seen, the seventh letter, a 'V', and the fourteenth letter, a 'C', have been interpolated. These extra letters are a totally meaningless jumble. They obviously constitute a hidden message of some sort and indeed will be analysed later. For the moment, the awareness of this large number of additional letters is all that is necessary to grasp the significance of the next step in the thought process of the decipherment.

With a coded text available in the scores of extra letters, it is possible to take the Alpha and the Omega as indications that most of these letters are smoke-screen. Perhaps the actual message is concealed between these two, which signify 'Beginning' and 'End'.

An examination of the text between the Alpha and the Omega shows that we are back on familiar ground. Again there are readily visible raised letters, as in the 'Dagobert' message. Between the Alpha and the Omega there are five letters raised above the line of writing, each separated by six letters from the next:

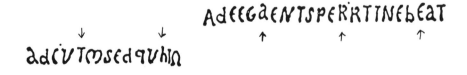

If this A R E T H is the message hidden between the Beginning and the End, it seems to be not very helpful. Even so, it leads one to seek more raised letters, and a further seven are, in fact, to be found preceding the Alpha, and also separated from each other by six letters:

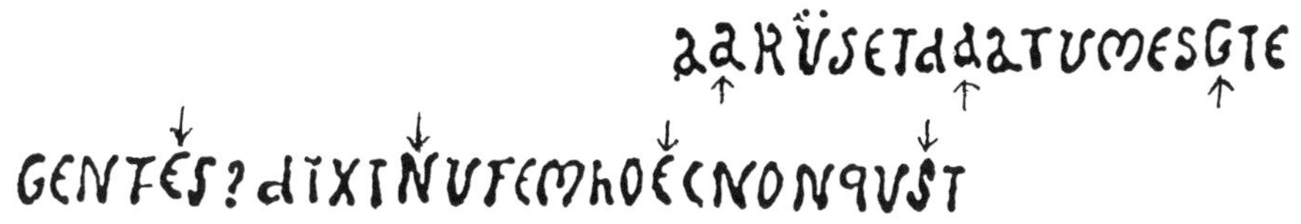

ᴌᴌᴋᴠ̈ᴊᴇᴛᴅᴅᴌᴛᴠᴍᴇꜱɢᴛᴇ

ɢᴇɴꜰᴇ́ꜱ�?ᴅ̄ᴉxᴉɴ̃ᴠꜰᴇᴍʜᴏᴇ́ᴄɴᴏɴꞯᴠꙅ̃ᴛ

This additional group – A D G E N E S – completes a meaningful phrase: AD GENESARETH, 'To Genesareth'. (Lake Genesareth or Tiberias, the Sea of Galilee, which figures so significantly in the New Testament.) This phrase, too, could function as a key word to a complex cipher.

In finding these raised letters it is inevitable that the letters **A** and **Ω** have already stood out clearly to the decipherer as being dropped below the lines of writing. One must therefore hunt for further dropped letters. The first is to be found at the end of the fourth line of text. It is a 'P'. One letter is dropped in each of the following four lines: A N I S. Next come the dropped Alpha and Omega and then, in the first, second and fourth lines following are S A L. The lowered letters therefore give us PANIS AΩ SAL – 'Bread and Salt' – separated by the Beginning and the End. Yet another possible key word.

The decipherer now has four key words which may unlock the code contained in the meaningless jumble of interpolated letters, but here also lies the first smokescreen. Any attempt to use these keys will prove fruitless as well as enormously time-consuming. They are a superb distraction for the hunter after complexities. Much more important, the inevitable desire to make sense of the secret message in the interpolated letters is itself a most effective distraction from another layer of brilliant simplicity which is embedded in Parchment One.

The parchment itself provides all that is necessary to make the next vital step. But a helpful indicator is to be found in another piece of evidence known as the Dalle de Coume-Sourde. (See over page.)

The inscription is said to have been carved on a stone found a couple of miles from Rennes-le-Château, near to a place called Coume-Sourde. As with all the other pieces, the provenance of the drawing is uncertain and the stone (if it ever existed) is now lost. The Latin is ungrammatical, which renders it so ambiguous as to be of no certain or practical use. However, the inevitable attempt to wrench a meaning

27

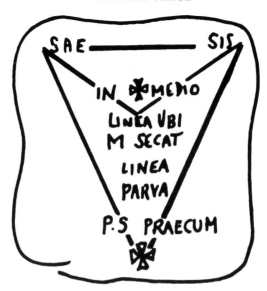

from the text is again a useful distraction from the extremely simple geometric design which surrounds it:

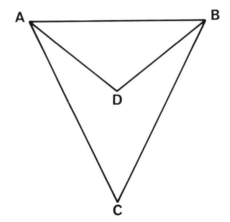

A triangle A–B–C with two lines intersecting at D. This is the first clear glimpse of geometry, and it is echoed in the small device in the top left corner of Parchment One:

The parchment also has three apparently meaningless crosses in lines 4, 7 and 10. They do not act as punctuation and seem to serve no purpose.

Here the code-maker displays the subtlety of his genius. If the right question is asked, a clear answer is revealed. The first and most obvious question is: what will happen if lines are drawn to connect the crosses? For this experiment it would seem best to choose the crosses in lines 4 and 10, as a line connecting them will pass through a minimum amount of the written text. Immediately upon making the attempt it is clear the correct decision has been made. The line passes through three letters only: S I and O. With a rule laid across the page, it is obvious that this line should be projected, and it will be seen to slide between the letters 'O' in the last two lines to terminate on the 'N' in the bottom line:

This repetition of the familiar key word 'Sion' is the code-maker's confirmation that the correct path has been chosen.* Drawing lines to link the other cross produces no significant result. What, then, is the next step along the path?

From this point on, the reader may find it interesting to lay a sheet of tracing paper over the reproduction of the parchment and draw in the fascinating under-layer of the document, for it will show not only the incredible ingenuity of the man who created these secret messages but

* It may be noted that the 'I' of 'SION' is, in fact, the letter 'T' of the word 'AUTEM'. This does not invalidate the reading. A careful examination of the text will show that 'T' has been deliberately written for 'I' on more than one occasion.

also demonstrate the way in which the decipherer is sometimes forced down certain lines of thought with a beautiful and inexorable logic.

The triangular device at the top left and its relationship with the three crosses suggests the possibility that something resembling the geometry in the Coume-Sourde Stone might be present. The upper face of this small triangle can be seen to be projecting in the direction of the cross in line 4. A straight edge will confirm this fact. The lefthand face of the triangle is also angled directly towards the base of the line which revealed the 'Sion' key word. With these lines drawn in, the parchment now exhibits the triangle A–B–C, but lying on its side. (Point C is the tip of the triangular device.)

The line A–D is simple to find. The cross in line 4 (point A) is joined to the cross in line 7. The line B–D is more interesting. There is no cross, no precise point, to aim for when projecting the line from point B. There is, however, in roughly the correct place, the gap before the last letter of line 2 – the only isolated letter in the text. But a gap is not precise in the way that a cross is precise. A moment's contemplation shows that the gap is at the approximate mid-point of the line A–C. Choosing the exact mid-point (which falls in the gap) gives the necessary precision and the 'Coume-Sourde Stone' pattern is now complete.

That is not all. The searcher has been led to choose the exact mid-point of a line; has been made to find it, and therefore to consider its possible significance. It follows that a circle centred on this mid-point will naturally pass through the two outer points A and C. The designer of this extraordinary puzzle again confirms that this is exactly what is intended. Drawing this circle with a pair of compasses produces a satisfactory and convincing result. The remaining two crosses, those in lines 7 and 10, are found to be lying precisely on the circumference of this circle.

The final step is to centre a circle of the same radius on the intersection of the lines at point D. Points A and B will be seen to fall on the circumference, which also accounts for the third face of the small triangular device. Joining the points where projections of the lines A–D and B–D cut the circumference produces this fascinating design:

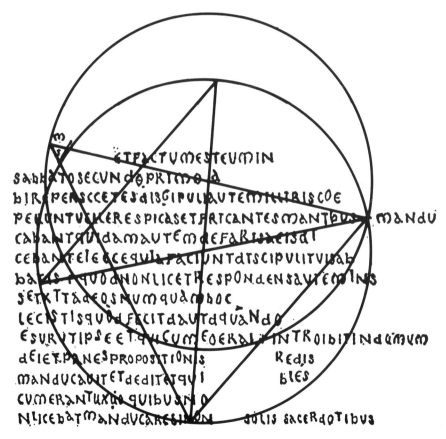

And it is on to this complex geometric pattern that the Latin text has been carefully overlaid.

In following these steps the reader will have confirmed that this design is not in any way imaginary, but is clearly and carefully structured into the document. The geometry was unquestionably of prime importance to the creator of the ciphers. What was he trying to convey?

When the design was first found in 1971, the story was still firmly rooted in the mystery of a buried treasure. Only subjective guesses were possible. Perhaps the clearly visible circle and crescent were meant to represent the astrological and alchemical signs for the Sun and the Moon – gold and silver? There was also the slightly disturbing fact that the five-pointed star – the pentacle – was breaking through its surrounding circle. This, too, had implications in the realm of magic and the occult. As any reader of Denis Wheatley is aware, when a magician wishes to raise spirits, he does so within the protective girdle of a Pentacle. To break the circle is to allow the evil to enter. These and other unprovable suggestions were made in attempts to explain the significance of the pattern in the parchment. There seemed to be an undercurrent of such imagery in the clues. The imagination was too easily tempted to run into murky by-ways. The code-maker was certainly trying to say something though, as yet, his voice was muffled.

3

Whispers on the Wind

The parchments have provided the first glimpse of the Pentacle, but they are, of course, not the only clues. We are told that Saunière was led to immense wealth. Whatever might have been the source of his riches, he was lavish in his generosity. He is credited with financing the four kilometre new road which replaced Rennes-le-Château's dirt track down to Couiza in the valley below. He paid for a water-tower to provide piped water to each house in the village. He built a handsome villa with a crenellated tower in the garden to house his library. He also redecorated the village church.

It was in this last gesture of munificence that he seems to have succumbed to the irresistible urge to play the Barber of Midas. The flamboyant imagery with which the tiny church is crammed is Saunière's equivalent of 'whispering on the wind'. With what seems a sort of impish humour, clues have been scattered both inside and outside the building. Some of them are, perhaps, smoke-screens, some are red herrings, while others are vague and ambiguous. Although there is nothing to match the superlative clarity and logic of the parchments, some of the clues are startlingly ingenious and precise, once their language is understood.

The warning note is sounded as soon as the church is entered. Crouched inside the doorway, a hideous and deformed devil lies in wait – not the conventional figure to find as welcome to a place of Christian worship. Beyond the devil, the church is crammed with a phantasmagoric mass of detail. Yet, for all the garish near-vulgarity of

33

Bérenger Saunière on the day of dedication of his extraordinary redecoration of the village church.

the florid decoration, nothing is obvious enough to attract more than fleeting attention. Casual visitors will see no more than they expect to see, albeit treated in a somewhat lurid style. Even the grotesque devil in the doorway has an apparent justification. However, 'for those with ears to hear and with eyes to see', he demonstrates how, in this place, layer after layer of meaning is buried beneath a seemingly innocent surface.

The devil statue supports above his head a scallop shell which is filled with water. This is the benitier, the Holy Water stoup, which every visitor to a Catholic church expects to find near the entrance. In a small cartouche above the Holy Water are the initials 'B S' – and why indeed should not Bérenger Saunière mark with his initials the work on which he had lavished so much care and expense? Crowning all, there are four angels, each of whom makes a gesture which is an element of the Sign of the Cross, the action performed by the pious once they have dipped their fingers into the Holy Water. Between the angels who make the Sign of the Cross and the devil is written the phrase 'By this sign ye shall conquer'. Thus there is a surface sense to

 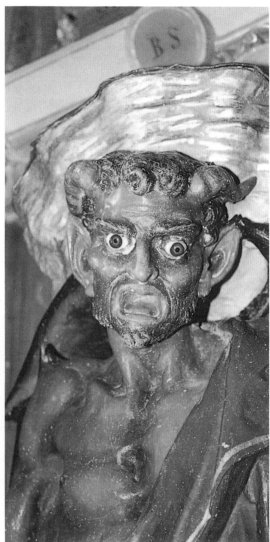

satisfy the unwary, though Saunière nudges one to look again. 'By this sign ye shall conquer' is often to be seen in Latin: 'In hoc signo vinces'. When it appears in French, it is 'Par ce signe tu vaincras'. In his church Saunière has added one tiny word: 'Par ce signe tu le vaincras' – 'By this sign ye shall conquer him'. Again, nothing glaringly exceptional . . . 'him' obviously refers to the devil beneath. It is enough to draw the informed eye to make a more careful examination.

The devil statue is half-squatting in an uncomfortable, twisted pose, almost as though he were sitting. But where is his chair? On a hillside to the south-east of Rennes-le-Château is a large rock carved into the shape of a great throne. It is known as *Le Fauteuil du Diable* – 'The Devil's Armchair'. Can one be sure that Saunière is drawing attention to this *Fauteuil du Diable*?

The devil's right hand makes a confirmatory gesture. The thumb and forefinger are curved into a precise and neat 'O'. Just a few feet from the Devil's Armchair, a tiny spring bubbles from the hillside. The spring is called *La Source du Cercle* – 'The Spring of the Circle'. Saunière's devil does indeed seem to be indicating a precise place. Even so one must beware. The treasure-hunter will all too easily be tempted to scamper away on a wild-goose chase in search of gold and jewels, but we are not engaged upon a treasure hunt. We are simply listening to voices from the past.

For the treasure-hunter, there are more indications of place to be found in the church. One more concealed in the Devil statuary group will suffice as example. The 'B S' already noted as Saunière's signature above the Holy Water stoup has also been read as an indication of the confluence of two local rivers, the Blanque and the Sals. Where their waters converge, a small and gentle whirlpool is formed. It is known locally as Le Benitier – 'The Holy Water Stoup'. Is the searcher to stumble from the river in the valley to the Devil's Armchair on the hillside in search of whatever an avaricious mind may imagine? Or is one to think, to wonder, and to look further?

The startling significance of this statuary group of Devil and angels is concealed beneath these surface implications, these apparent references to local features. The clue to this deeper meaning lies in what appear to be nothing more than simple pieces of decoration. Between the Holy Water and the angels are two curious and unreal little beasts. These beasts are salamanders, who were supposed to be born out of fire, to be elemental spirits of Fire. Now at last the imagery sharpens into focus. The angels are creatures of pure spirit, or Air; the Devil is Rex Mundi, Lord of the Earth. The group is composed of symbolic elements. The Devil (Earth) supports the Water, which in turn supports the salamanders (creatures of Fire), and crowning all are the angels (creatures of Air).

Earth . . . Water . . . Fire . . . Air. The four elements of all Hermetic thought – of astrology, of alchemy. It is, to say the least, unexpected to find erected in a church in the first years of the twentieth century, the symbolism of the mediaeval quest for the Philosopher's Stone. For most people today, after all, the alchemist was engaged upon a fanciful search for a mysterious, quasi-magical substance which would convert base metals into gold and confer eternal youth. What is Saunière saying? Is he attempting to distract the searcher with the claim that his wealth was produced by Alchemy? Or is he turning us back towards the past, to another time, to another way of thinking?

The church is filled with such whispers. Statues, paintings and stained glass all contain curious details which seem to be asking to be interpreted. Such interpretations, though, may be nothing more than fictions in the mind of the eager interpreter. All too easily, meaning can be found where none was intended. Certainty is an elusive quarry. But one of Saunière's hints proves clear and significant. It is a pointer on the path of discovery. For this reason it must be explained in detail.

*

All Catholic churches contain representations of the fourteen Stations of the Cross, portrayals of the principal incidents of Christ's journey to Calvary. They always depict the same events in the same sequence. Station I, for example, is always 'Pilate washes his hands'. Station VI is always 'St Veronica wipes the face of Jesus'. Station XIV is always 'Jesus is laid into the tomb'.

The manner of portraying these incidents can vary greatly. In some churches the Stations are beautifully executed and realistic paintings, in others they are simplified almost to abstraction, occasionally indeed they are reduced merely to the numbers I to XIV written in sequence around the church. At Rennes-le-Château the Stations of the Cross are elaborate and detailed, in keeping with the florid style of Saunière's entire decorative scheme. Arguments have been made against the validity of any interpretation drawn from these strange pictures. These objections are based on the fact that at least two other churches (notably nearby Couiza) have Stations with certain features identical to those at Rennes-le-Château. As the basic scenes are built around moulded groups of figures, it is not too surprising to find that these moulds have been used more than once. The important differences, however, lie in additional features which have been added by Saunière. Indeed, the figures at Couiza are simply presented as plain silver against empty gold backgrounds, whereas Saunière's backgrounds are filled with painted details.

Innumerable questions are raised by even a superficial examination of these fourteen pictures. In Station I, for example, Pilate washes his hands but why does he wear a veil? Prominent in the background is a man who looks away from the scene and raises his hand above his head.

Clasped in that hand is an object which appears to be a golden egg. What relevance can this figure have to the story of Christ's Passion?

Dominating the foreground of Station II is another total irrelevance – a young man who bends to pick up a stick. In Station VIII the figure of a child is clad in a garment whose pattern seems to be that of a Scottish Tartan. In Station X a hand rests on the wood of the Cross, but this hand is unrelated to any of the figures who are depicted in the scene. Can such untoward oddities be simply the decorative embellishments of the artist? Perhaps – though in Station VI a clear message has been deciphered.

The first hint is in a blatantly irrelevant background detail. A soldier in the top left corner turns his back and holds his shield up against the sky. The gesture is as strange as it is meaningless, and yet it is the first element of a precise instruction which Saunière wishes to give. Here is another example of the incredible ingenuity which has been employed

to communicate information in a cryptic way. In this game, the sounds of words are used to convey a double sense. In Station VI, the elements of the message are to be defined in as simple a way as possible and then one must listen to the words.

There is no briefer description that can be given to the feature in the top left corner than 'high shield' – in French, *Haut Bouclier*. The shield partially obscures a tower of which it is possible to see only half – 'half tower', *demi tour*. The principal element of the picture is 'Veronica with the cloth' – *Veronica au lin*.

Also noteworthy is the figure on the right, who is Simon of Cyrene, the bystander who helped Jesus by carrying His cross. Simon is not looking at the scene before him; his gaze is fixed upward and outward towards something else. Simply stated: 'Simon is looking' (*Simon regarde*). There may be other elements which, when defined, could augment the message, (the background dome, for example), but the four elements already selected convey a clear instruction in the following way:

HAUT BOUCLIER pronounces precisely the phrase AU BOUT CLIER, which means 'at the bottom of the enclosure'. ('Clier' is an archaic French word for enclosure, modern French using the word 'clôture'.)

DEMI TOUR has a double meaning. It is not only 'a half tower'; it also means 'a half turn'.

VERONICA AU LIN falls into two ingenious parts: VERS HAUT NID and KAOLIN. The first part means 'towards the high nest'. 'Nid d'aigle' (eagle's nest) is a description commonly used in French to denote a dominating mountain feature. A mile or so from Rennes-le-Château and towering on the eastern skyline is the Mountain of Cardou, which is composed of china clay, or 'kaolin'. Thus VERS HAUT NID KAOLIN means 'towards the high china clay peak' – Cardou.

SIMON REGARDE is simply saying CIME ON REGARDE – 'the crest one is looking at'.

The message is now complete: 'Au bout (du) clier, (faites un) demi tour vers (le) haut nid (de) kaolin. Cime on regarde.' – 'At the bottom of the enclosure, make a half turn towards Cardou. One is looking at the crest.'

It would be possible to argue that this has been merely an amusing attempt to squeeze meaning from the meaningless were it not for the fact that the message makes absolute sense on the ground. In Rennes-le-Château there is only one enclosure – the cemetery. Entering by the only gateway, one can follow the instructions precisely. It is possible to walk 'to the bottom of the enclosure' and make 'a half turn' which indeed faces one directly 'towards Cardou' . In clear confirmation of the message, there is 'a crest' very clearly visible in the middle distance. It is the crest on which stands the ruin of the Castle of Blanchefort. Saunière seems to be pointing to this crest as being of importance.

When this decipherment was made in 1971, it was to prove extremely productive and certainly helped to point in the right direction. However, there is a further double entendre in the French which, even if it had been noticed at the time, would have been meaningless. Later in this investigation, Saunière's message will assume a slightly different and much more illuminating meaning.

4

Poussin Holds the Key

At this point in the investigation, when preparations were under way for a brief twenty-minute item in a 'Chronicle' programme, the mysterious 'we' for whom de Sède spoke, decided to add fresh fuel to the fire. A letter arrived from de Sède which contained the detailed workings of the major cipher concealed in the interpolated letters of Parchment Two. The unravelled message was extraordinary:

BERGERE PAS DE TENTATION QUE POUSSIN
TENIERS GARDENT LA CLEF PAX DCLXXXI PAR LA
CROIX ET CE CHEVAL DE DIEU J'ACHEVE CE
DAEMON DE GARDIEN A MIDI POMMES BLEUES.

SHEPHERDESS NO TEMPTATION THAT POUSSIN
TENIERS HOLD THE KEY PEACE 681 BY THE CROSS
AND THIS HORSE OF GOD I COMPLETE (or I
DESTROY) THIS DAEMON GUARDIAN AT MIDDAY
BLUE APPLES.

Even more extraordinary was the coding system which had been used to conceal the message. The system was unbelievably complex and seemed to go far beyond the requirements of mere concealment. There seemed almost to be an element of initiative test or ritual contained in the tortuous steps which the decipherer was required to make. (Full details of the mechanics of this code are to be found in Appendix One.)

With the decipherment, de Sède included the information that the code had been broken by cipher experts of the French army, using computers. After carefully checking through the details of the coding system, I found de Sède's explanation unconvincing. Did he really believe the computer story? Or was he simply passing on what he had been told? Being ignorant of code-breaking procedures, I made enquiries of British Intelligence. Here, too, de Sède's claims were treated with scepticism. 'Whoever unscrambled this message', I was told, 'must be in possession of the key and full details of the system.' The cipher was the most complex that my informant had ever seen and would, he insisted, have taken months of work to prepare. Without the keys and cipher system the code must be considered 'utterly unbreakable'. 'It does not present a valid problem for a computer.'

Whoever had given the information to de Sède, or by whatever other means it had come into his possession, the decipherment was unquestionably correct. As far as the 'Chronicle' film was concerned, the problem remained to elicit some sense from the bizarre message. Nothing in it seemed coherent or meaningful, apart from the opening words: SHEPHERDESS NO TEMPTATION THAT POUSSIN TENIERS HOLD THE KEY. Here, at least, was a pointer, vague though it might seem to be.

However, a tiny passing reference in *Le Trésor Maudit* presented an apparent connection. According to the book's account, Saunière had taken the parchments to Paris to be examined by experts. Before returning to his village, the priest had called at the Louvre Museum where 'he bought reproductions of three paintings – *The Shepherds of Arcadia* by Poussin; *St Anthony Hermit* by Teniers; and a portrait of Pope Celestin V. A strange assortment.' In the book this had seemed no more than an irrelevant snippet of information, evidence of nothing more than the supposed depth of the writer's research. But now it seemed legitimate to ask if Saunière had bought the reproductions because the paintings were relevant to the ciphers. 'Shepherdess' linked with Poussin in his *Shepherds of Arcadia*, and 'No temptation' seemed to link Teniers with *St Anthony Hermit*. De Sède insisted that the relevant painting was *The Temptation of St Anthony*, but as there were numerous versions of this by David Teniers as well as by his son, David Teniers the Younger, there seemed no way of being certain which Teniers painting might be the relevant one.

There was also the slightly curious reference in the secret message to 'no temptation'. What could this imply?

Later research suggested that the relevant Teniers painting might well not be a *Temptation of St Anthony*, but rather *St Anthony and St Paul in the Desert* – the only Teniers painting to depict the Saint NOT being tempted. However, the original of this picture is now lost, so effectively blocking this line of enquiry.

The remainder of the secret message, with its references to 'daemon guardian' and 'blue apples' has led to much speculation but little else. It would be pointless to enumerate all the many tortuous meanings which have been read into the message, ranging as they do from the highly sophisticated to the totally absurd. Again, the sophistication of one's approach to such a problem, creating the expectation of complexities, tends also to create difficulties where none perhaps exist. It is possible that the problems in the hunt for sense in the message may arise simply because a meaning is being sought in something which is meaningless. While this is admittedly as much an hypothesis as any other put forward, it does at least seem to have the merit of being realistic. It is important to consider the nature of the code-maker's problem.

There was a message to convey and the chosen medium was the gravestone memorial to Marie de Négri. In creating the puzzle, certain pieces were already defined. Her name, for instance, could be played with only in a very limited way. On the other hand, there was no absolute necessity to give her age, nor to omit her date of birth. Neither was REQUIESCAT IN PACE obligatory. Another pious phrase would have done equally well, or it could have been omitted altogether.

Thus it can be seen that certain elements of his puzzle were within the encipherer's control and some were not. With this in mind, it is not difficult to see how, in juggling with the text of his message and the imposed limitations of his medium, he would have been left with a certain number of redundant letters. What, for instance, was he to do with all those 'X's in the date? Perhaps, therefore, the enigmatic BLUE APPLES and other curious parts of the message are simply a wry means of using up the unavoidable extra letters. Alternatively, it is possible that these obscure references, while pertaining thematically to the central message, do not actually illumine anything or constitute concrete clues. Indeed, to seek a meaning in the entire text would seem fruitless and to be asking the impossible of even this code-maker's amazing ingenuity. Even so, it would be difficult to support this hypothesis were the message consistently obscure throughout. But it is not. The first sentence is quite clear:

BERGERE PAS DE TENTATION QUE POUSSIN TENIERS GARDENT LA CLEF.

The essential statement that 'Poussin and Teniers hold the key' is unambiguous.

While the 'Chronicle' team was pondering the relevance and possible meaning of the new decipherment and how it would affect the film, de Sède, or his masters, decided that we should be given further food for thought. A second letter arrived with the astonishing news that a tomb which resembled the one in the Poussin painting had been identified near to Rennes-le-Château. Photographs and exact details of the location would follow, de Sède informed us, 'as soon as he had them'.

Clearly, what had seemed a story of purely local significance was now growing into something of much greater importance. The 'Chronicle' producer, Paul Johnstone, decided to abandon our twenty-minute item in favour of a full-length programme. Filming was postponed in order to give me more time to research and augment the material. While I awaited de Sède's further details, I returned to a more careful examination of the decipherment of Parchment Two.

5

Here Lies the Noble M

Without the appropriate information for creating a computer programme capable of taking the irrational and unconnected steps which
the decipherment requires, how would it be possible to identify the
key? Four possible key words have already been presented to the
decipherer: 'REX MUNDI'; 'AD GENESARETH'; 'PANIS AΩ SAL'; and 'SION'.
Certainly a computer could be used to try each of them in turn, but
when these are found to be useless, how is the correct key to be
discovered? How is the decipherer to know that the keys (for there are
two) are not in the parchments at all? Only with instructions from the
master code-maker would it be possible to take the next step. Now,
with the details provided by de Sède, I knew that the keys lay in the
inscriptions on the gravestones of Marie de Blanchefort.

Like the cryptic imagery in the church, the inscription on the
headstone presents a superficial sense to satisfy a casual examination;
straightforward and conventional enough, albeit there are numerous
minor oddities in the wording which have been attributed by some to
the illiteracy of the stone-carver. But the wary searcher has already
learned that it is to such oddities that one must turn attention – and
almost every line has an anomaly of some sort:

i.   The words CI GIT ('Here lies') have been written as CT GIT –
      a 'T' has been inserted in place of an 'I'.
ii.   The last letter of NOBLE has been written with a small round 'e'
      and not a capital letter.

CT GIT NOBLe M	HERE LIES THE NOBLE
ARIE DE NEGRᵉ	MARIE DE NEGRI
DARLES DAME	D'ABLES DAME
DHAUPOUL Dᵉ	D'HAUTPOUL DE
BLANCHEFORT	BLANCHEFORT
AGEE DE SOIX	AGED SIX
ANTE SEPT ANS	TY SEVEN YEARS
DECEDEE LE	DIED THE
XVII JANVIER	SEVENTEENTH JANUARY
MDCOLXXXI	1781
REQUIES CATIN	MAY SHE REST IN
PACE	PEACE

iii. The 'M' of MARIE has been separated and left behind on the preceding line.

iv. The last 'E' of NEGRE is smaller than the other letters. This word is also mis-spelt and should be NEGRI. Thus in this case there is a small square 'E' instead of an 'I'.

v. DARLES should read DABLES. An 'R' instead of a 'B'.

vi. The last letter of the fourth line is again a small square 'E'.

vii. In the seventh line, the 'P' of SEPT has been dropped out of place and is again a small letter.

viii. In the Roman numerals for the date 1781, an 'O' has been written instead of a 'C'.

Thus there are eight indicated letters in two groups: four large – 'T', 'M', 'R', 'O' – and four small – 'e', 'EE' and 'p'. The four large letters can be formed into one French word, and one only – MORT, 'dead' or 'death'. The small letters also can only be made into one word – épée, 'sword'. In addition to these eight anomalies, the 'T' has been omitted from the name HAUTPOUL and the words REQUIESCAT IN PACE have been incorrectly divided. The omission of the letter 'T' proves to be an inevitable outcome of the mechanics of the cipher, but it is worth pointing out that the incorrect break in the words REQUIESCAT IN PACE produces the French word CATIN – 'Whore'! An extraordinary error to find inscribed on the tomb of a noble lady. It does, however, serve as a reminder that the church of Rennes-le-Château is dedicated to St Mary Magdalene, the repentant harlot who figures in the Gospel text into which the cipher is embedded.

The eight clearly visible anomalous letters which spell MORT EPEE are, however, the necessary first key to the decipherment. The headstone has begun to yield up the secrets hidden beneath its innocent surface message. The grave-slab has thus far remained mute. There seems to be not even a simple superficial sense to the carved inscription. Yet there are obvious links with the other pieces of evidence.

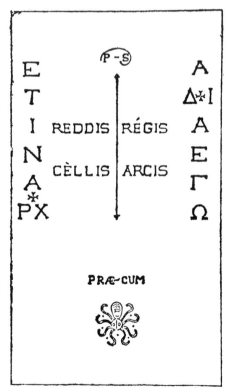

There is the monogram 'P–S' which has already appeared on Parchment One. The Coume-Sourde Stone also bears the letters P.S in association with PRAECUM. On this slab, P–S and PRAE-CUM are linked by a vertical double-headed arrow.

The entire inscription can be broken into three components for examination. First of these is the clear block of Latin text in the centre, which is the only part to be readily readable:

REDDIS	REGIS
CELLIS	ARCIS

The second group is formed by the 'P–S' monogram linked with PRAE-CUM and with the curious spider-like creature at the bottom beneath it.

The third component is the two vertical columns of letters which frame the central block.

The decipherment of this stone will demonstrate several of the different sorts of game played by the creator of the messages.

First, then, the Latin phrase: REDDIS REGIS CELLIS ARCIS. As with the Coume-Sourde Stone, this is unclear, ambiguous Latin. There is also the vertical line which divides the words into two groups and makes it possible to read the phrase either horizontally or vertically. Latinists will without difficulty be able to translate the phrase in a number of different ways. For example, REGIS can mean either 'you rule' or 'of the king'; REDDIS can mean 'you give back' or, taking the background story into account, could be simply 'Reddis', one of the earlier names of the village. Of the several interpretations possible, only one seems to make any sort of helpful sense: 'AT ROYAL REDDIS (Reddis of the King), IN THE STORE-ROOMS OF THE FORTRESS'. This raises the question: 'what is at Royal Reddis in the store-rooms of the fortress?' An answer is provided by the second component of the inscription which is formed by the 'P–S' monogram linked to the PRAE-CUM plus 'spider' element of the gravestone inscription at the bottom.

The single word 'praecum' as written on the Coume-Sourde Stone is meaningless, but here it is broken into two syllables by a hyphen, 'prae', meaning 'before' or 'preceding'; 'cum' meaning 'with'. The looped line surrounding the 'P–S' monogram clearly begins before the letter 'P' and, curving round, terminates before the letter 'S':

In the familiar manner of playing childish games, one can interpret the line as indicating something which precedes P and precedes S. Alphabetically, 'P' is preceded by O and S is preceded by R. *Or* is the French word for gold!

Thus the 'Prae' part of PRAE-CUM has enabled a sense to be elicited from the P–S monogram. The 'cum' part now implies that we must link what we have found 'with' ('cum') something.

The arrow-headed vertical line visually links the top of the inscription to the bottom, where the spider-like creature is to be found. Here is another example of the coding game already encountered in 'Veronica with the cloth'. Again, one must play with the sounds and meanings of words.

The French word for spider is *'araignée'* – thus, the two parts of this component resolve to *'Or araignée'*. Spoken aloud – and especially with the thick regional pronunciation of the Languedoc – the sound is almost exactly *'Or à Rennes'*. This makes a different sense and completes the meaning of the central body of the inscription: 'The gold at Rennes is at Royal Reddis in the store-rooms of the fortress.'

Interesting and apt as this decipherment may be, I must here confess that, having made it, I have no faith whatever in it! There seems here to be a dangerous possibility of having induced the evidence to conform to a pattern which is not necessarily valid. It is very tempting in this sort of hunt, if only subconsciously, to produce the answers that one expects to find. Furthermore, 'P–S' is evidently an indicator of the Priory of Sion. It is also possible to argue that the spider-like creature is even more like an octopus – which plays havoc with the interpretation. However, the reader is free to accept it. The code-maker may even have wanted people to do so. Red herrings abound in the waters of Rennes-le-Château, and this is but a small fry providing more fun than confusion. The third component of Marie de Blanchefort's grave-slab has a much more solid and significant indication to make.

E	A
T	Δ✠I
I	A
N	E
A	Γ
✠ PX	Ω

The righthand column is clearly Greek, but it is quite meaningless. The lefthand column could again be bad Latin. It might, for example, be possible to read the line as ET IN PAX ('and in peace') but this is grammatically incorrect, and unhelpful too.

In fact, the two columns of writing conceal a most significant phrase, hidden in a very simple fashion. It would be well here to remember that, until comparatively recent times, the peasant population of this area would have been almost entirely illiterate. Of the very few who could read, even fewer, if any, would have had a knowledge of Latin or Greek. Such learning was indeed restricted SOLIS SACERDOTIBUS, 'only to the priesthood'. Here, every priest's knowledge of Latin need be augmented by no more than a superficial acquaintance with Greek. The columns of writing simply display a Latin phrase, but written in a form of the Greek alphabet. The letters need merely to be changed from one alphabet to the other. E – T – I – N and A are common to both alphabets. But the Greek 'P' (Rho) is the equivalent of R; X is K (or hard C); Δ is D; Γ is G; Ω is O. The phrase can now be read. It is ET IN ARCADIA EGO. And these are the words which are written on the tomb depicted in Poussin's painting of *The Shepherds of Arcadia*.

It should be noted that, on the grave-slab, the phrase is broken into two parts. The lefthand column provides only ET IN ARC which, on its own, means 'and in arc'. The slab has already provided the sentence: 'The gold at Rennes is at Royal Reddis in the store-rooms of the fortress'. 'And in arc' could well be a continuation of that sentence, (though ADIA EGO would then cease to have any meaning). However, the possibility that ET IN ARC should be interpreted as 'and in arc' is by no means unlikely.

When de Sède's further details arrived, we learned that the tomb of Poussin's painting could be found some four miles to the east of Rennes-le-Château. It was not far from a Château called Arques!

6

Shepherds of Arcadia

Within days of the arrival of de Sède's letter, I was driving slowly along the road which leads eastwards from Rennes-le-Château and Couiza. Beside me were the photographs which de Sède had sent with the information that I would find the structure to the right of the road between the villages of Serres and Arques.

The road is a beautiful one, winding past the massive shattered ruin of the Castle of Coustaussa, then beneath the Crest of Blanchefort and the soaring china-clay Peak of Cardou. The hillsides above the road are richly wooded, dense and mysterious. The landscape has a brooding atmosphere, not speaking so much of darkness and of menace as of a quiet self-contained strength. One can believe that such a country can hold its secrets very tightly to itself. Beyond Cardou, the road passes the uncompromising square block of the Castle of Serres; then, a mile further, a tiny group of houses clustered above and to the left – the farmsteads of Peyrolles and Pontils. Here the road begins a long and gentle curve, skirting a tiny ravine to the right. Across the ravine, perched on a knoll and clearly visible from the road, is the Tomb of Poussin's painting, or rather, it was visible until April 1988, when it was demolished by the owner in a misguided attempt to fend off the assaults of grave robbers. Nothing now remains but a sad and insignificant scattering of rubble.

I feel the burden of my own share of responsibility for this regrettable act of destruction. The attention which I and other writers have drawn to this story in books and in films has made the tomb familiar to

55

people around the world. Numbered among them, sadly, are mindless and irresponsible treasure-hunters who have battered senselessly at the stones in search of something which exists only in their avaricious and deluded imaginations. Indeed, the very first assault on the tomb occurred on the afternoon of my first day's filming at the site in 1971. The beleaguered owner was eventually forced to erect barbed wire and numerous 'Keep Out' signs, but with little effect. Although the innocent visitor could still see and enjoy the scene from the public highway without need for trespass, this was evidently not enough for the gold-obsessed vandals. At last came the crowning folly of an onslaught with explosives. Hardly surprisingly, the owner wished to put an end to such lunacy, which he did with a sledgehammer.

There was no treasure buried here. As the records show to those who take the trouble to consult them, and as the sacrilegious assaults had laid bare, the tomb contained nothing but two coffins. These held the bodies of the wife and the mother of an American, Louis Lawrence, who had owned the site during the 1920s. When he opened it for the first of these family burials, the tomb was empty. The destruction of the monument, regrettable as it is, has at least assured the quiet and undisturbed rest of the Lawrence ladies.

Even now, with the tomb no longer completing the picture, one is immediately struck by the extraordinary precision with which Poussin has rendered the landscape which forms the background to his Arcadian scene. Behind the knoll, in the middle distance, is the rock of Toustounes. Further to the right is the flank of the mountain of Cardou and then the unmistakable silhouette of the crest of Blanchefort. Most satisfactory and exciting of all is to recognise the distant outline of Rennes-le-Château which is visible as an insignificant mound on the far horizon to the right. That mound is exactly placed in the painting. Poussin has painted Saunière's village in its exact relationship to the knoll at Pontils.

The accuracy of Poussin's rendering of the landscape does not prove that the tomb existed in his time. As usual, there are those who claim to 'know' that the tomb was erected in the early years of the twentieth century. Such knowledge does not constitute proof. Even if it did, there always remains the possibility that the monument was constructed in imitation of Poussin's invention and to complete the picture. For no argument against the relevance of the structure can overcome the detailed exactitude of the background.

When I first stood before the tomb and realised that I was gazing at

Cardou

Blanchefort

Rennes-
le-Château

Poussin's marvellous Arcadia, I was neither surprised nor puzzled. After all, many artists have painted careful and detailed views of real landscapes. I was delighted by the discovery and, once back in London, sought the advice and guidance of the acknowledged world-expert on the life and works of Poussin. This was Anthony Blunt, then Director of the Courtauld Institute of Art and Surveyor of the Queen's Pictures, later disgraced for his treasonable activities.

I thought that Blunt would be interested, perhaps even excited by this new and fascinating contribution to our knowledge of the painter's work. I was quite unprepared for his total unwillingness even to consider the evidence. 'This is a mere coincidence,' Blunt said, 'an extraordinary coincidence, but a coincidence nevertheless!' He expressed no interest even in investigating the matter further. I confess that I found such a closed-mind attitude utterly incomprehensible, though I have since learned that this is a not uncommon trait in the more pompously self-opinionated experts in many fields. Any discovery made by an outsider seems to them to be *ipso facto* valueless.

Blunt insisted that *The Shepherds of Arcadia* was the depiction of a purely imaginary tomb in a purely imaginary landscape. This is what he had been taught and this is what he continued to teach. The Voice of Authority – his opinion – was not open to question. He must be right; it followed, therefore, that my contradictory suggestion must be wrong. I pointed out that even minor details in the picture suggested the contrary. The rock upon which the righthand shepherd rests his foot is in its exact place. The tree behind the tomb was identified at Kew Gardens as 'possibly *Quercus ilex*' (the holly oak), an ancient specimen of which grows in precisely the correct spot. All these 'coincidences' suggested to me that Poussin must have visited the location, or at least have seen very detailed sketches. 'Impossible,' said Blunt. 'Poussin did not work from such sketches. And he never visited that part of France.'

I questioned whether, after three centuries, even an expert could be so dogmatic about the whereabouts of an artist throughout his entire life. 'Yes,' Blunt insisted. 'Poussin's career was extremely well documented.' Almost his entire working life was spent in Rome, apart from one period of two years during which he was in Paris as Painter to the Court of King Louis XIII. Poussin arrived in Paris in December 1640 and was back in Rome in November 1642. As Blunt himself had told me that *The Shepherds of Arcadia* was painted 'about 1640', this coincidence of dates seemed to me to be another possible confirmation of my theory. Blunt remained adamant: 'Poussin never visited this part of France!' I asked for details of the route taken by the artist on his journeys between Rome and Paris. 'He took the usual route,' was the response. When I pointed out that this was not an adequate reply to my question I was told 'he took the route that everybody took.' The end result of my enquiries showed that nobody knows the route taken by Poussin on that significantly timed journey. In face of such weak counter-arguments, the possibility remains that, on his way to or from

Paris, Nicolas Poussin for some reason made a brief detour into the Languedoc and the fruit of that detour was *The Shepherds of Arcadia*.

The weight of Blunt's reputation would have been sufficient to crush my amateur's opinion were it not for the fact that other hints existed, hints that Poussin was engaged in some strange and shadowy activity. One of these hints is in the form of a letter sent on the 17th April 1656 from Rome to Paris. The letter was written by the Abbé Louis Fouquet who had just paid a visit to Poussin. It was addressed to Louis' brother, Nicolas Fouquet, who was Superintendent of Finances at the court of Louis XIV. The relevant part of the text is as follows:

> . . . M. Poussin . . . et moy nous avons projetté de certaines choses dont je pourray vous entretenir à fond dans peu, qui vous donneront par M. Poussin des avantages . . . que les roys auroient grande peine à tirer de luy, et qu'aprés luy peut estre personne au monde ne recouvrera jamais dans les siècles advenir; et, ce qui plus est, cela seroit sans beaucoup de dépenses et pourroit même tourner à profit, et ce sont choses si fort à rechercher que quoy que ce soit sur la terre maintenant ne peut avoir une meilleure fortune ni peut-estre esgalle . . .

> . . . M. Poussin . . . and I discussed certain things which I shall with ease be able to explain to you in detail. Things which will give you, through M. Poussin, advantages which even kings would have great pains to draw from him and which, according to him, it is possible that nobody else will ever rediscover in the centuries to come; and what is more, the matter involves little expenditure and could even be turned to profit, and these are things so difficult to discover that nothing now on this earth can prove of better value nor be its equal . . .

Blunt admitted that this letter had never been properly understood by art historians. It was, however, his opinion that the letter concerned a commission for ornaments for Fouquet's garden. He was unable to explain how such a commission could bring 'advantages which even kings would have great pains to draw from him', nor how the ornaments could be 'so difficult to discover that nothing now on this earth can . . . be its equal'.

Poussin had certain things to communicate – things 'of value' – and presumably Nicolas Fouquet learned their secret from his brother. Fouquet's subsequent history can legitimately provide grounds for speculation concerning the nature of this secret. He had become immensely wealthy while managing the Royal Exchequer and eventually his life-style began to rival even the King's in splendour. In 1661 he was removed from office and imprisoned. When he died nearly twenty years later, his two servants were ordered to be kept locked up in isolation. Their gaoler was instructed: '. . . You shall lock up both of them in one room, from which you will be able to assure His Majesty that they will have no communication with anyone either by speech or in writing.' These orders were issued because it was suspected that they might know 'the majority of important matters of which M. Fouquet was cognisant'. It is also reported that the King personally went through Fouquet's papers. Not long after, the King acquired Poussin's *Shepherds of Arcadia*. It was not put on public display, but was kept locked away in 'le petit appartement du roy'. None of this, of course, proves that Fouquet's downfall was in any way linked with the secret communicated by Poussin. Nevertheless, the evidence seems to indicate that Poussin's painting of the tomb and the tomb itself were somehow linked to a secret, and that secret would seem to relate to the mystery of Rennes-le-Château.

All the same, these were still no more than hints and possibilities. I lacked certainties. I contemplated the painting, enjoying that magical Arcadian tranquillity with which Poussin had invested the scene and marvelling more and more at his precision. I became convinced that this picture was, in some way, one of the keys of which the ciphered parchments spoke. But what message was Poussin trying to convey? The correct answer to that question, I was sure, would be unambiguous, unarguable, not reliant upon subjective interpretation. And I had also learned to watch for apparent anomalies.

In the painting, the Rock of Toustounes is precisely placed, but the landscape to the left of this feature is depicted as a descending slope. In reality, the hillside rises to the left. Poussin has painted a cloud, however, which mirrors the silhouette of that rising hillside – Berco Grando. Why, I wondered, should he have made that alteration? Had he originally painted the mountain and then decided to change it to cloud? This was a question easily resolved in the laboratories of the Louvre Museum. In due course X-rays of the painting showed that no major alterations had been made. Poussin had intended from the outset to paint the descending slope exactly as we see it. I could make little certain progress down this particular line of investigation.

Nevertheless, the X-ray of the painting was, fortuitously, to provide the indicator which led to the next discovery. As I examined the fascinating under-layers of paint, my attention was drawn to an oddity, an almost unnoticeable detail which is quite invisible to the naked eye.

Below is a detail from the X-ray, showing the head of the shepherd on the right of the picture.

The X-ray makes it possible to see through the laurel wreath which binds the shepherd's brow. Revealed beneath that wreath is the under-painting which shows that point where the shepherd's staff cuts across the line of the tomb. The extraordinary fact revealed by the X-ray is that the staff DOES NOT cut across the tomb! On the contrary, one can clearly see that the painting of the tomb is overlaid upon the staff. This can mean only that the staff was painted before the tomb.

The painting of foreground details before background seems an unusual procedure, suggesting that the staff was in some way a critically controlling feature in what Poussin was attempting to do. Alternative arguments may be put forward to explain away the anomaly, but they cannot affect the discovery to which it led. An important breakthrough had been made. Attention had been drawn to the shepherd's staff.

*

A search for complexities will serve only to generate complexities. Experience has shown that the route to a provably valid discovery is found by choosing the simplest possible approach. One of the simplest statements that can be made about the shepherd's staff is that it is cut in two by the shepherd's arm. Measurement with dividers will show that the division is exact. Moreover, that exact measure is repeated from the top of the staff to the tip of the shepherd's pointing finger. It is also repeated in the division of the lefthand shepherd's staff, which is bisected by the line of the kneeling shepherd's back. A straightforward check, maintaining this half-staff measure, will quickly produce numerous repetitions of this fixed distance between significant points in the painting. This discovery was a clear indicator that there was an unexpectedly rigid geometry underlying the composition of *The Shepherds of Arcadia*. In fact, so rigid is this framework that one marvels at Poussin's ability, working as he was in such an utterly restricted way, yet to achieve a masterpiece of such fluidity and harmonious repose. The artist's genius enables him to transcend his self-imposed geometric strait-jacket. However, I was to learn that the concealed substructure was not an idiosyncratic invention of Poussin's.

The new discovery had moved the enquiry far beyond my amateur's competence. Professor Christopher Cornford of the Royal College of Art had made a particular study of the geometrical structure of paintings and had, indeed, already analysed one of the works of Poussin in this way. He agreed to undertake an analysis of *The Shepherds of Arcadia*.

According to Professor Cornford, every old master painting he had investigated conformed to 'fairly straightforward geometric and/or arithmetic subdivisions of the rectangle'. There were two basic types of system – one 'was based on the account of the creation given in Plato's *Timaeus*, and was published by Alberti in his *Ten Books on Architecture* (Florence, 1485). It proceeds by calculation as much as by construction using instruments, and it had great appeal in the High Renaissance and its aftermath, since it both dissociated art and architecture from the old, manual masonic tradition of mediaeval times, and associated them with humanist scholarship. Moreover the number system used was a kind of invocation of the divine inasmuch as the building or painting became a microcosmic rehearsal of the primal act of creation.'

The other type of system was the masonic-geometric. According to Professor Cornford, this was 'incomparably the older of the two, indeed it seems to have been known to the Ancient Egyptians and to our own megalithic culture. It survived, often surrounded by an atmosphere of craft (if not cult) secrecy, until Alberti's time, and subsequently went into eclipse . . . '

Poussin, it would seem, should be expected to construct his paintings in conformity with the Albertian-Timaean system and indeed, Professor Cornford found evidence of this. But, as he worked on his analysis, he was surprised to find evidence of the older and long-outdated masonic-geometric system. 'I would have expected Poussin to have associated himself with the Renaissance Philosophy in this matter rather than to have used the older method. I was also surprised at the degree to which it was possible to conform with both methods simultaneously, almost like a musician writing in two keys at once and making them both harmonise. An extraordinary feat of virtuosity. And I was frankly surprised at what seemed to me the quite staggering rigorousness and exactitude with which Poussin seemed to have observed both of the constructions that he used, but rather particularly the second (older) one . . . '

What had so startled Professor Cornford was not my 'half-staff' measure, but something which seemed unconnected with it. The ancient geometric symbol which Poussin had used was the Pentacle.

My search for significant geometry had begun when I found the pentacle concealed in the Rennes-le-Château parchment. And now here it was again, controlling Poussin's depiction of the landscape within which that parchment had been found. With his awareness that I was then, in a certain sense, searching for the 'X' on a treasure map, Cornford offered a suggestion. 'If Poussin is saying anything of this nature,' he said, 'he seems to be saying that pentagons . . . and their

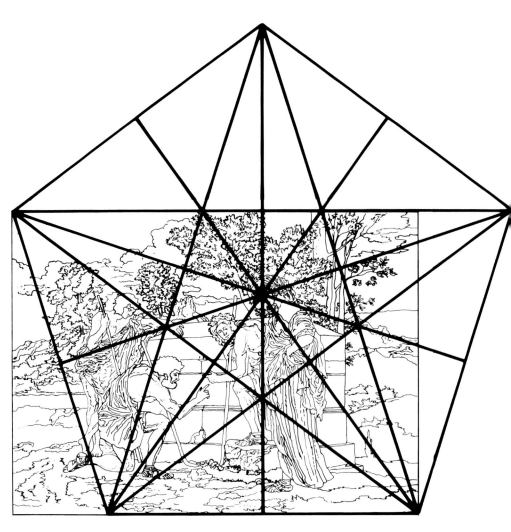

constituent angles are very much involved. Would it be worthwhile testing the map?'

The master code-maker had taken enormous pains to lead the decipherer towards pentagonal geometry and to encipher his message that 'Poussin holds the key . . . '. Professor Cornford had found the lock into which that key fitted.

7

The Key Turns

The suggestion that pentagonal geometry might be found on the map raises two points for consideration. First, such lines on the ground must, of their very nature, be suspect. When found they are often no more than the subjective result of the researcher's attempts to find them. A Glastonbury Zodiac is as easily conjured as pictures in a fire. It cannot be disputed that if a straight line be drawn for a great distance across country, then a number of apparently interesting points are bound to be found upon it. To prove which of these points may be coincidental and which have been deliberately aligned would seem to be a well-nigh impossible task. Impossible, that is, unless some other consideration renders the alignment meaningful in an objectively provable way. Even then the finding of such an objectively provable alignment would not necessarily explain its purpose.

Second, and not linked in an immediate and obvious way with alignments, is the question: what makes a place holy?

Fifteen hundred years and more before the birth of Christ, sites like Stonehenge in England and Carnac in France were seeing the construction of enormous and complex structures of ritual and religious significance. Why were they placed where they were? Perhaps for no other reason than that the site was convenient and facilitated the construction. Thus a place may become endowed with holiness because a centre of worship has been placed upon it. This has certainly become true of many places that could have been arbitrarily chosen. But could there also be places of which the reverse is true? Could there have been a holiness which was already inherent in the site itself? Was there, in some places, a thing which could be venerated and so require the construction of a temple on the already sanctified site? Was not this the principle governing the sacred groves of classical antiquity, or Apollo's shrine at Delphi? Even in Christian terms, the same principle obtains. For example, the cave which was supposedly the tomb of Christ and witnessed His resurrection is venerated and has become a place of worship.

The idea of alignments and the idea of holy places might go together in the context of a culture – such as that which produced Stonehenge – to which the timing of certain events was important; heavenly events, that is, which were regular and so could be calculated.

As a suggestion, therefore, of what could make a place holy, and so a suitable site for a centre of worship, one might postulate the discovery by an early culture of a site – a hill-top, an island, a crag – which was so placed in relation to another natural feature as to provide a significant alignment, so that, when viewed from the chosen site, the sun rose – for example on mid-summer day – precisely behind a nearby crag. Here, then, would be a place where the gods had provided a natural indicator of a celestial event. The site once found, it would not be difficult to erect additional convenient standing stones or other features which, when viewed from the key spot, would all serve to indicate other similarly significant events. A place with two or perhaps even three natural features all providing significant alignments would be very much rarer, and so more holy.

Thus prefaced, it is now possible to return to Professor Cornford's suggestion that alignments should be sought in association with the mystery of Rennes-le-Château, and more specifically, those associated with the angles of a pentagon. With this suggestion in mind and a knowledge of the countryside around the village, it was not difficult to decide where to begin the search.

Three principal mountain features in the immediate locality, each of them relevant to the mystery and on each of which a castle had been built, seemed to be placed in the relationship of the triangle A–C–D in the diagram below. These three sites are: A – the Templar Château of Bezu; C – the Château of Blanchefort; D – Rennes-le-Château. A check on the map of the area proved that these three castles are indeed in this exact relationship.

Each castle is on a natural mountain top. The distance from Bezu to

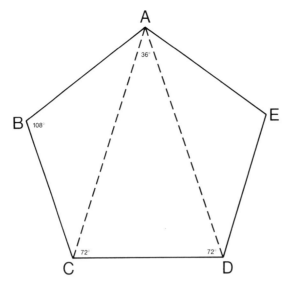

Rennes-le-Château is exactly the same as that from Bezu to Blanchefort. The coincidence of these natural features being so accurately placed is astonishing. So remarkable is the exactitude of the geometry, so precisely linked are the angles with the Poussin pentagon that there could be no doubt of the relevance of this discovery to the mystery. Further investigation of this freak of topography was clearly of prime importance.

With no great expectation of success, it was decided first to extrapolate the two missing pentagonal points from the triangle already found. The angles were measured, the distances matched and the lines drawn. The result was scarcely to be believed. Each of the other points is also upon a natural mountain feature. No structures appear to have been built upon them, but each is marked on the map with a 'spot height'. (These are indications of high points provided by the map-makers – in this case the French Institut Géographique National.)* The eastern point (point B on the above diagram) falls on a hill called La Soulane. The spot height is marked as 587m. The western point (point E) is on the end of a rising crest – the Serre de Lauzet. The spot height is 559m. Here is a gigantic pentagon, some fifteen miles in circumference. The great symbol is laid out on the ground, and for those with eyes to see – for the initiated – it is clearly discernible from Rennes-le-Château. At night, a fire lit upon each peak would easily be seen.

* Spot heights are convenient references to elevation, they are not necessarily the highest point in the vicinity. In the case of La Soulane and the Serre de Lauzet, however, they are the high spots. Trig points (as on La Pique and the mountain of Cardou) are also height indicators where physical markers have been placed.

The clues surrounding the mystery had led ineluctably toward this discovery. Those clues had stressed the importance of the pentagon, and here it was, fashioned of mountains by the forces of nature. For our remote ancestors, such a phenomenon would clearly be the work of the gods. But what was its significance?

The best-known answer to that question is magic. The pentacle, the five-pointed star enclosed within a circle, is the age-old symbol that was used by magicians for the raising of spirits, or of the Devil. Today, magic has become a matter for ridicule, or has been relegated to the lunatic fringe. But this story has a very long past and the blood of thousands has been shed in the fight against witchcraft. Even now there are many who take magic all too seriously, no matter how much other people may scoff. The very word occult has come to be associated only with magic, witchcraft, devil worship. But occult simply means 'hidden' – a secret body of knowledge reserved only for the initiated. In that sense, the discovery at Rennes-le-Château was certainly part of what would once have been occult knowledge. Nevertheless magic was only partially satisfactory as an explanation for the mystery. Saunière's story, for all its strangeness, had not been trailing a scent of satanism. The clues left by him and by his predecessors had implied rather more something mystic, religious, perhaps heretical but certainly not evil. And of course there was the hint of treasure, which had always seemed to me to be too overtly an attraction away from the truth rather than towards it. With the discovery of the pentacle of mountains came the necessity to find some way in which the mystery could link with the geometry, and it was quite obvious that such a link would not be found unless the modern, sceptical, scientific world-view were abandoned in favour of an attempt to see the world as our ancestors had done.

Of course, very little can be deduced with certainty concerning the attitude of early inhabitants of Rennes-le-Château to their village and its environs. However, a tiny and illuminating glimmer came from the church. Like the château, the village church dates back to at least the time of the Visigoths, some thirteen centuries ago. The church is dedicated to Saint Mary Magdalene, and Saunière drew additional attention to the hamlet's patron saint when he called his extravagant gothic library tower 'Magdala'.

Mary Magdalene was the redeemed sinner who was the first to see Christ after His Resurrection. Through her redemption from sin and her unique knowledge of the Risen Christ, she was regarded by the occult initiates of the Middle Ages as a medium of secret revelation. Those initiates had chosen the planet Venus as her symbol in the cosmos. In the thinking of those who created this mystery, could there have been a link between Mary Magdalene and/or the planet Venus, and the pentacle at Rennes-le-Château?

The early astronomers saw the Earth as the centre of the universe, around which the Sun, the stars and the planets revolved. Each planet forms its own pattern of movement around the Sun as seen from the Earth. For the ancient watchers of the heavens, those differing patterns of movement allowed them to draw geometric shapes based on the positions of each planet when it was aligned with the Sun. For instance, Mercury is aligned three times in its orbit and the pattern formed by these conjunctions is an irregular triangle.

Mars is aligned four times and forms an irregular four-sided figure. Each planet makes a different number of alignments and each forms its own irregular pattern. Only one planet describes a precise and regular geometric pattern in the sky – and that planet is Venus, the heavenly counterpart of the earthly Mary Magdalene – and the pattern that she draws as regular as clockwork every eight years is a pentacle.

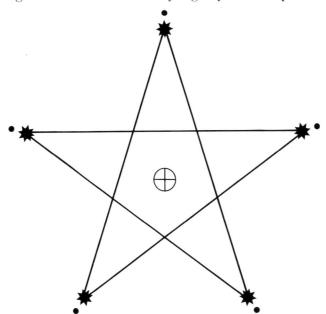

In the obscure writings of the old alchemists, cabbalists and astrologers there is a resonant phrase: 'As above, so below.' Here, indeed, was a link between the worlds of matter and spirit, between base and corrupt man here on earth and the twinkling firmament where dwelt

God and all His Saints. Mary Magdalene, the medium of a secret revelation, was herself the image of the secret revelation in the sky. At Rennes-le-Château, village of Mary Magdalene, lies the great pentacle of mountains, the earthly counterpart of the perfect pentacle in the heavens – the secret and hidden pattern of Venus, the Magdalene, each pentacle precise, known, yet hidden. One must be initiated into the Mystery before one can see the age-old, unchanging truth that the heavens find reflected in this tiny location on the face of the Earth. To the mediaeval mind, such an image was immensely powerful, immensely potent. In that majestic hidden symbol in the sky, harmonious, unchanging, regular as a metronome, was the music of the spheres.

With this discovery, one could begin to sense a link with an even older culture. Such a discovery would lie within the grasp of those more ancient astronomers, the builders of Carnac and Stonehenge. For them, too, the gods had here provided a holy place where there was a natural mirror of a celestial event. For Christians, Venus had become the Magdalene, and so the church was dedicated to her. For an earlier culture, Rennes-le-Château was a gigantic god-given Temple to the Mother Goddess.

8

A New Discovery

After the discovery of the pentagon of mountains the logical next step is the fixing of the centre. Without a knowledge of the five mountain peaks, the centre is impossible to find. With that knowledge, it is impossible to lose. Not even a map is necessary to identify the spot. One needs simply to possess the hidden knowledge of the five mountains. Here, indeed, would be the perfect place to hide something. For as long as the mountains stood, the location could never be lost. If, as one had been led to believe, the mystery was simply the location of a hidden treasure, then this would have been the end of the trail.

Lines were drawn on the map to fix the central point. Again the seemingly impossible happened. At the centre of the huge pentagon marked out by the five peaks is yet another mountain. It is called La Pique.

The exact geometric centre falls, in fact, on a steep scree slope on the northern flank of La Pique. Any disappointment that the centre does not fall neatly and precisely upon the crowning spot height of the mountain should be mitigated by a reminder that this is not an inaccurately structured pentagon but a well-nigh perfect natural phenomenon, owing nothing to human intervention. Six mountains arranged in so precise and meaningful a pattern – the odds against such a natural occurrence must be astronomical. It would be interesting to know of any other place quite like it anywhere in the world.

With the discovery of the sixth mountain peak one must now ask: was Saunière aware of this amazing freak of nature? Is the interpreted

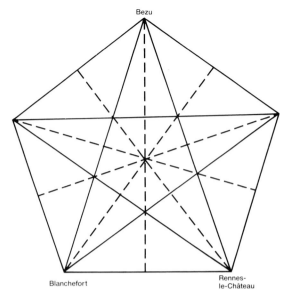

Bezu

Blanchefort

Rennes-
le-Château

phrase 'Simon regarde' not an attempt to convey this knowledge? I have rendered the phrase as 'cime on regarde', 'the crest one is looking at'. Should it not now be interpreted – and still with the same sound – as 'six monts . . . regarde', 'six mountains . . . behold!'

In making the discovery of the central peak, another piece of the jigsaw also falls into place. The centre of the pentagon lies a mere couple of hundred metres to the west of a farmhouse identified on the map as Coume-Sourde. On page 28 is reproduced the mysterious design allegedly carved on a stone which was found near to a place called Coume-Sourde. The newly discovered pentagonal geometry now enabled an informed guess to be made about this stone. Had it perhaps marked the geometric centre of the design? This was indeed the conclusion which I reached at the time of the discovery. Later revelations in this book will cause that conclusion to be modified.

Each of the three BBC films on Rennes-le-Château elicited a gratifying response. Viewers were fascinated by the story and mail flooded in. After the transmission of *The Shadow of the Templars* I was showered with a mass of excited and imaginative theories. Nevertheless, as I opened each letter, I hoped that someone might have seen something which I had missed – something demonstrable and provable. Many indeed were the claims to have solved the mystery, but most proved to be nonsense. The few which seemed sensible were rendered doubtful by the need to take one or other aspect of the solution on faith. There was little point, for instance, in assuring me that the cloud to the right of the central crag in Poussin's painting is really the depiction of a head. This is no more than a subjective

72

viewpoint, having as much validity as seeing a face in the cracks of a plastered wall or in the pattern of a wallpaper. Such discoveries are matters of opinion and, as such, are proof of nothing. For me, they can have no value.

Yet there was one viewer who made a genuinely provable discovery – and it was astonishing! David Wood, who was trained in topographical surveying, found another layer of complex geometry in the landscape of Rennes-le-Château. The next vital step had been taken.

Even more exciting was Wood's discovery that a number of the man-made structures in the area seemed to be conforming to some sort of pattern too. When he showed me the results of his research, I was impressed by the care and accuracy displayed in his working methods. Here, at last, was something which was, in my terms, demonstrable and provable. The geometry, the layout of the structures, the extra-ordinary new pentacle which he had identified, all served to convince me that an important breakthrough had been made. At the same time, Wood's work was marred for me by an occult, numerological and sexual interpretation which he had imposed upon the undeniable facts. When, for instance, his geometry developed crescent shapes, he did not hesitate to relate these to legends of Ancient Egyptian deities. Here, he claimed, was 'The Ark Crescent of Nut' and 'The Boat Crescent of Isis'. These shapes, in turn, developed further curving forms in which he could see 'The Womb' and 'The Vagina of Nut'. Nevertheless, I agreed to write a foreword for the book when he published his discovery in 1985 and sounded a clear cautionary note:

> . . . in all that I have to say about this book – I am concerned only with the demonstrable geometry, mathematics and measure which the author sets out. Of his conclusions and his interpretation of his evidence I have nothing to say.

In his book, *Genisis*, David Wood claimed that '. . . At last the age-old secret of Rennes-le-Château is solved.' In reality, however, he had only glimpsed a tiny fragment of what was waiting to be uncovered. He could so easily have made the next step and seen what was already before his eyes. Instead, he looked at the wonder – and then obscured it. This is a salutary lesson to those who would lead themselves towards their own pre-determined conclusions.

David Wood accepts whole-heartedly and sincerely the mystic

73

significance of certain numbers. He believes also that these numbers represent various gods of the Ancient Egyptian pantheon. The myths concerning these gods are, for him, the echoes of stories of a 'pre-Adamite civilisation' – a sort of super-race from Outer Space who created mankind. I can find no evidence to support such contentions. No evidence, that is, beyond the desire which some people have to believe them.

Where, for instance, I would find it interesting to note that two intersecting lines form angles of 72° and 108°, David Wood's thinking leads him to write:

> Here was the number of the goddess Isis (18) with her mother Nut (o) in attendance. Dividing these two numbers by 18 analysed their 'hidden' meaning: the first became 4 indicating the square or construction, the lineage of the temple walls: the second becomes 6 the number of the sun-god Ra . . . The numbers disclosed by the Isis factor acting on the meridian were 4 and 6 which when multiplied give the 24 hours of the day. And Osiris was there as well, for the 360° cycle, when divided by 24 gave his number before he was dismembered (15). (Genisis, p.67)

I am bound to say that I find this way of thinking fantastical, though I have to admit that it was this thinking which led David Wood to his undeniably valid discovery. I acknowledge the debt which I owe to him, and regret only that his own occult and Atlantean predilections prevented him from seeing the true nature and magnitude of what he had so nearly discovered.

In the kind of hunt upon which we are engaged, there is a paramount need for absolute objectivity. The evidence alone must guide the research. The researcher must look with the eyes of a child, seeing only what is there and not bending it in any way to suit a favoured theory. As soon as one 'sees' the gods of Egypt depicted in the evidence, then one is tempted to ignore other evidence which does not fit. In precisely this way, Wood ignored the original pentagon of mountains which had inspired his work. They did not conform to his geometry and so he dropped them from his thinking. Had he not done so, he might have come to the simple and obvious conclusion that there had to be more to his discovery than he had yet defined.

Subjective interpretation can lead into dangerous and sterile dead ends. Confronted by his own extraordinary discovery, Wood implied that the geometry which he had found could only have been achieved by 'aerial survey based on known ground control positions . . . In simple terms we decided it would be easier to say this was "the work of the gods"' (*Genisis*, pp.68–9). Easier, certainly. To see the work of 'the gods' or of a super-intelligence from Outer Space in these unexpected findings is simply to say 'I don't understand how this was done'. Such a 'solution' certainly avoids the necessity for any further research, and it must be admitted that huge numbers of people long for 'proofs' of this kind. For me, Outer Space is a lazy explanation.

So what, exactly, was it that Wood had found? In attempting to follow my own path through the labyrinth, I am obliged to restrict myself solely to those two fragments which undeniably form part of the Holy Place: his pentacle, and his partial identification of the measure used in its construction. In short, his discovery was made in the following way.

First, he was aware of an odd snippet of Rennes-le-Château lore: that on St Mary Magdalene's day (July 22), sunrise, as viewed from the church dedicated to her in the village takes place directly above Blanchefort. On his map he drew this line and was surprised to notice that its projection passed through the church in the village of Arques. He then discovered that a right angle to this 'sunrise line', struck at Blanchefort, would take him directly to the church in the village of Rennes-les-Bains.

His next step was to measure his 'sunrise line' between Rennes-le-Château and Arques church and note that this line was divided at one third of its length by the French Zero Meridian. (Prior to the adoption in 1884 of Greenwich as the International Zero Meridian, each country made use of its own. The French Zero Meridian – which will be discussed later – was apparently established in the seventeenth century and is still used on the official maps produced by the Institut Géographique National.) With brilliant foresight, Wood noted that the line is six English miles long and that the Zero Meridian falls at two miles. He also noted that the distance between the churches of Rennes-le-Château and Rennes-les-Bains is three miles.

A further coincidence brought in the Poussin Tomb, a site of obvious significance in the story. He noticed that a line drawn from Rennes-les-Bains church to the Poussin Tomb cut the 'sunrise' line exactly at the Zero Meridian. His next move, as he himself says, 'was either inspired or just plain lucky'. He projected the line from the

Poussin Tomb to Rennes-les-Bains southwards by exactly one mile and arrived at a point which I shall designate 'X'.

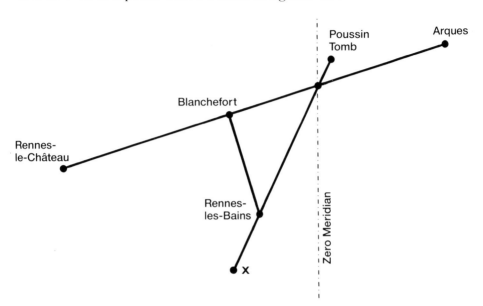

(Here I must make a brief digression from Wood's work in order to tidy away a loose end. I have previously noted that the Coume-Sourde Stone was supposedly found near to a place with that name. I questioned whether it had marked the geometric centre of the pentagon of mountains, which lies to the west of Coume-Sourde Farmhouse. Point 'X', arrived at by David Wood, is about half a mile to the east of the farmhouse, but it does lie close to a small stream which is also called Coume-Sourde and from which the farm takes its name. Point X may therefore also, possibly, be the original location of the Coume-Sourde Stone.)

What, then, is the significance of Point X? Incredibly, it is *exactly* equidistant from the churches in the villages of Rennes-le-Château, Coustaussa, Bugarach and St Just-et-le-Bezu and from the Château of Serres. It is also very close to the same distance from the church in the village of Cassaignes. One must accept either that this is the most unlikely of all coincidences – or that those structures were deliberately placed in exact relationship to Point X! X is the geometric centre of a circle of major buildings some six miles in diameter! In addition to this extraordinary circle, Wood's map-trained eye was also able to find some further alignments between structures which produced this astonishing new pentacle.

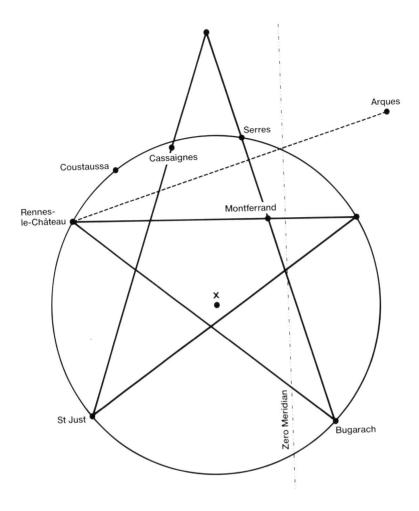

In an echo of the original discovery of the pentacle in the parchment, this one, too, breaks through its surrounding circle. This new pentagonal figure is extraordinarily complex. Each of the five outer triangles surrounding the inner pentagon is a perfect isosceles with two equal faces, but each one is different. Without the structures on the map as guide, the figure would be extremely difficult to draw – even on paper. To achieve it over miles of mountainous terrain, and without the aid of sophisticated modern surveying techniques, is a breathtaking feat which makes the building of the Pyramids seem relatively straightforward. David Wood, who found it, believes that the work was executed by a 'pre-Adamite' super-race from Outer Space who used 'aerial survey from fixed ground positions'. Oh, that the answer – and the discovery – were so simple!

Christopher Cornford enabled me to turn the key in the lock; David Wood pushed open the door. Now we shall take the first few faltering steps through that portal. All that has been revealed so far, marvellous though it is, is no more than a glimpse into a tiny ante-chamber. The unseen and unimagined vastness of the Temple lies beyond.

*

The new discovery had shown that there was a controlled placing of structures in conformity with a complex geometry in the country around Rennes-le-Château. Undeniably impressive as this discovery was, I found it unsatisfactory. I was puzzled by the fact that the original natural pentagon of mountains seemed to play no part in the developing design. True, Wood had noted that La Pique, the central mountain, lay exactly on the line of his pentagon which ran from Rennes-le-Château to Bugarach. But, apart from this passing reference, his book ignores it, and no attempt is made to relate the hill of La Soulane or the Serre de Lauzet or the Templar Castle of Bezu into his geometry.

Something was going on around Rennes-le-Château and that something was geometrical and specifically pentagonal, as Professor Cornford had suggested. For me, it was associated in some way with the pentacle of mountains, and now also with a number of the man-made structures in the area. The map, I was sure, would reveal much more than had yet been seen.

There were also other fragments in the saga of Rennes-le-Château that were beginning to ring very faint bells in the deeper recesses of my memory. After fifteen years immersed in the Saunière mystery, my mind was filled with innumerable odd and unexplained curiosities which had surfaced from time to time, only to recede when nothing could be found to link them firmly to the story. One such fragment was a seemingly crazy book written by Saunière's friend and neighbour, the priest of Rennes-les-Bains, Edmond Boudet.

9

Fixed by an English Mile

In 1886, Boudet published a tome called *La Vraie Langue Celtique* – 'The True Celtic Tongue'. This book is wildly confusing and, for a native English speaker, unintentionally but hilariously funny. Boudet's thesis is that all languages derive from one universal tongue, spoken by the sons of Noah before Babel . . . and that language was English! Or rather, Anglo-Saxon, as spoken by the race of Celts. According to Boudet, a group of Druids rushed about the world giving names to everything in sight. These Druids were known as the Neim-heid which (in English) reveals their task: they were the Name (Neim) head (heid). God, naturally, spoke English. Having created the first man, He was constrained to call him Adam as He found it necessary to 'Add [a] Dam' . . .

Boudet further gives numerous parallels between Anglo-Saxon and the dialect of Languedoc. He finds, for instance, that 'barata' means barter; 'bouich' means bush; 'counta' means count; 'bolo' means ball. All very impressive. One must, however, sense a doubt when he finds the Languedoc word for a mercenary to be 'préfaïthié' – which he equates with prizefighter!

St Augustin, too, derives his name from this remarkable Ur-tongue. Boudet tells us that Augustin 'certainly merited the name Eagle of the Assemblies which was so felicitously given to him'. Thus 'Aug', or hawk (a sort of eagle), and 'ustin', or hustings, which, as he informs us, is 'an assembly room'. Another particularly delightful example of Boudet's dotty theory is to be found in his interpretation of the language of the Berber tribes of Kabylia in Algeria. The Berber, he tells us, has great respect and admiration for the French. In their language, a Frenchman is called 'aroumi' and, as Boudet marvellously reminds us, 'roomy' in English means 'big' – and so 'great'. One can't help wondering how complimented a Frenchman might feel if an awe-struck Berber were to inform him: 'Monsieur, I think you're roomy.'

What has this harmless lunacy to do with the mystery of Rennes-le-Château? Boudet provides a hint in the book's sub-title 'And the Cromlech of Rennes-les-Bains'. After regaling the reader with 223 pages of linguistic tomfoolery, Boudet devotes the last 80 or so pages of his book to a careful exploration of what he considers to be a complex megalithic structure spread over the countryside around his village. He even provides a map, though it seems to be of questionable accuracy.

However, Boudet is certainly trying to convey *something*. Is one to absorb his curious method of playing with words and then to interpret his description of the 'Cromlech' by the same method? This possibility struck me as too vague and uncertain in its results, and yet the book appeared to have a vital significance for many who buzzed around the honeypot of the treasure of Rennes-le-Château. De Sède had stressed its importance to me at the very beginning of my researches. And in the late 1970s, a couple of facsimile reprints of the book were published in France, one with a teasing preface by Pierre Plantard de St Clair.

I felt that *La Vraie Langue Celtique* could not simply be dismissed as the work of a harmless crank. The erudition which Boudet demonstrates in his pages hints that he had a well-trained and complex mind which would not be given to playing useless games. Boudet may yet have much to tell us, but I have gleaned only one indication from him which makes sense. Moreover, it seems to confirm David Wood's partial (and valid) discovery of a unit of measure. This one glimmer is all that I can present to the reader from Boudet's *magnum opus* and I do so because, whether or not my interpretation is correct, the conclusion will prove unquestionably to be the right one.

In making my habitual attempt to avoid the complex and to seek out only the simplicity of the material, I realised that while Boudet was demonstrating a complex 'game', he was basing it on a simple, if quaint, premise that the original universal language was English.

I found it impossible to accept the idea that all our primitive forebears should have developed the same spoken tongue, but in considering that concept, I realised that something which might be termed a universal language does indeed exist. It is Number. One or two or three notches on a stick, or scratches on a stone, would denote one or two or three no matter what language might be spoken. One is always one and two is two. With this absurdly simple idea, I progressed to the thought that Measure was a straightforward derivative of Number. A stick cut to a particular length could be used to indicate a distance, or a multiple of that distance. Measure, too, could be conveyed in a universally understood manner – and David Wood seemed to have identified a unit of measure.

Boudet was saying that the original universal language (Number? Measure?) was English. Wood's unit of measure was the mile . . . the English mile. Is this what Boudet was trying to convey? Is this the next discovery to be made, that his Cromlech was built to the English mile?

The idea is so bizarre that one is tempted to reject it out of hand – to say 'I don't believe it!' But I have long since learned never to close my mind to any possibility, no matter how unlikely it might seem. To say 'I don't believe' *without any evidence* is to make as much an act of faith as is made when one says 'I *do* believe'.

The possibility that Boudet's Celtic Stone Age Cromlech might be built to the English mile requires no act of faith either way. Here was a premise which I could test. What could I learn of early measure?

*

Before the late eighteenth century, units of measure appear to have been more or less arbitrary. The Romans preserved fixed measures which served as standards for the whole of their civilised world, but with the fall of the Roman Empire those standards were lost. Over the centuries since, innumerable measures have been defined in what seems largely haphazard fashion. In sixteenth century Germany, for instance, a 'lawful rood' could be arrived at by stopping at random any sixteen people as they left church on a Sunday morning and making them place their left feet one behind the other along a line. One sixteenth of the 'rood' thus arrived at would be considered 'a right and lawful foot'. There was a time when the English yard was fixed as the distance between the tip of Henry I's nose and the end of his extended thumb. In the thirteenth century, the inch could be defined as three dry barley-corns placed end to end. Our mile is said to have derived from the Latin *mille passus* – a thousand paces – a pace being a double stride of about five feet. Until the sixteenth century, the mile

The 'fixing of a lawful rood' from a woodcut in Jakob Kobel's *Géométrie* (1531).

seems to have had variations of as much as 800 yards. It was not until 1593 that Parliament established our 'Statute Mile' of 8 furlongs or 1,760 yards.

In 1791, the French National Assembly decided to adopt the metric system in an attempt to fix, once and for all, a verifiable measure which could be independently checked against a natural and unchanging 'standard'. The expertise then existed to make this possible, and so the metre was defined as one ten-millionth of a quadrant of the earth's surface; that is, the distance from the pole to the equator. This measure, verifiable and checkable on the earth's surface, was apparently the first system to be fixed in this way. Other measures, such as the English mile or furlong, pole or yard, were not so fixed. We believe they were defined in a purely arbitrary fashion.

My work on the Temple of Rennes-le-Château, however, seems to leave no doubt that the apparently arbitrary English measure (as Boudet has hinted) stems from a standard unit fixed in the remote past. Moreover, that unit seems to relate directly to the earth's surface, PRECISELY as does the metre. This, of course, implies that, at some early date, the devisers of the standard unit were able to measure the earth with accuracy. Maybe it is not surprising that no hint of such a contention has ever been heard by the public from any expert in the field, yet this very idea has been lurking in the scholarly literature for decades.

In his book *Historical Metrology*, published in 1953, A. E. Berriman ends his Preface by saying: '. . . the earliest mathematical texts . . . should be studied . . . to sharpen opinion on the right answer to a particular question: Was the Earth measured in remote antiquity?' Berriman goes on to quote many examples of ancient measures which seem to relate to precise divisions of the earth's surface. 'The English acre', he tells us, 'is the most intriguing of ancient measures because it is virtually equal to a hypothetical geodetic acre defined as one-myriad-millionth of the square on the terrestrial radius: if both acres are expressed as squares the difference between the lengths of their sides is less than 1 part in 1,200. The geodetic acre can also be defined as measuring one myriad square cubits in terms of a hypothetical cubit equal to one-ten-millionth of the terrestrial radius, and . . . its former existence is as plausible (or as incredible) as a cubit derived from the sexagesimal division of the Earth's circumference.'

When Berriman says that such a suggestion is either 'plausible' or 'incredible', he seems to be saying with admirable caution: 'Please don't expect me to make the decision. Here are the facts. Let somebody else risk having the egg slapped into his face!' As a layman and non-expert, I have no need to share his timidity. His evidence seems to me to be quite convincing. But Rennes-le-Château had led me to the conclusion long before I knew of Berriman's work.

When I became convinced that the mile measure was certainly being used in the layout of the churches in the Rennes-le-Château area, I was faced with an apparent anomaly. How could this precise measure have been employed when the churches were built upwards of a thousand years ago? Still more difficult to accept was the idea that the layout might have been fixed even earlier, in Celtic/megalithic times. I wondered if there might have been a much earlier measure in use from which the mile could have been derived. As I wandered into this apparent by-way in my researches, I stumbled upon a most extraordinary string of coincidences concerning measure that reminded me of Ian Fleming's dictum (which I slightly misquote): 'Once is chance. Twice is coincidence. But three times is enemy action!' Here was 'enemy action' to an alarming degree!

The definition of the Cromlech Measure which follows is no more than a corollary to my discoveries concerning the Holy Place of Rennes-le-Château. It is hardly my place to provide a detailed thesis on the history and development of measuring systems. Indeed, such a thesis lies far beyond my competence. However, this corollary must be presented in order to assist in the exposition which is to follow. It is my intention to present my findings in such a way as to be comprehensible to the educated lay-person while, at the same time, imploring experts in this field to verify what I have found. And to explain it, for I have not found in any published work on metrology the same type of proof which I shall here present.

This does not mean, of course, that such a publication does not exist – and if I am going over 'old ground' for metrologists, I apologise. I can only plead that what follows was new to me – and to everybody else to whom, so far, I have shown it.

*

The relevant pieces of my jig-saw were Boudet's (presumably megalithic) cromlech and Wood's (presumably English mile) measure. I was aware of Professor Alexander Thom's work, in which he established that the great Neolithic and Bronze Age stone circles were carefully laid out using a measure which he had termed the 'megalithic yard' of 2.72 feet. (It has been suggested that this measure may have derived from the *shusi*, an ancient Sumerian measure of 2.75 feet.) Dr B. K. Roberts, in *An Historical Geography of England and Wales*, refers to the work of other scholars producing further ideas and confirming Thom's work, and goes on to say:

> It is clear that Neolithic communities possessed great skill in civil engineering and organization . . . The idea of such intellectually sophisticated practices raises many questions and . . . [there is a] contradiction between the clear evidence for mathematics and astronomy on one hand and the negative evidence for recorded numeracy on the other.

In other words, the megalithic stone circles demonstrate that the ability was there, even though no written explanatory records exist. As will be seen, the Rennes-le-Château discovery will unquestionably confirm the sophisticated ability of its designers. Its corollary – the measure which they used – will demonstrate that those designers were using a unit which survives in the English measure.

Fixed by an English Mile

In attempting to verify the use of the English mile in the Rennes-le-Château cromlech, I was soon made aware that subdivisions of this unit were also needed. My attention turned to the 'Pole' (also known as the Rod or Perch) as one of the interesting possibilities. Like other measures in the historical past, the pole has shown variations. The accepted definition of a pole is now 5.5 yards – one 320th part of a mile, i.e. 198 inches. It would seem that this curious fraction of our arbitrary mile measure has never been considered to relate to anything other than the internal logic of its own system. It has certainly never been considered to relate in any way to the circumference of the earth, as the metre does.

Be that as it may, while I measured and re-measured upon my map I began to wonder if our present pole, having shown numerous slight variations in the past, is not a rounded-down version of an earlier unit, which I shall call the Cromlech Pole. I suggest that this Cromlech Pole was very slightly longer than the present definition of 198 inches – the difference being rather less than half an inch, in fact .41874 of an inch – and that this hypothetical Cromlech Pole of 198.41874 inches is as precisely related to the circumference of the earth as is the metre. For simple proof of this, the calculations must remain firmly fixed in Boudet's antediluvian English measure. The kilometre – one thousand metres or one ten-thousandth of a quadrant of the earth's surface – when translated into English measure is 39,370 inches, and the square root of 39,370 is 198.41874!

This might be nothing more than a startling coincidence were it not that there is an ancient Chinese measure called the Kung (or official) Ch'ih, the length of which is given as 14.14 inches – or, to within about one twentieth of an inch, the square root of 198.41874!*

There is more. The suggested origin of Professor Thom's Megalithic Yard is the ancient Sumerian Shusi, given as 2.75 feet. This is 33 inches, or exactly the one sixth division of a Pole.

Therefore: the SHUSI times 6 equals the POLE;
the KUNG CH'IH equals the square root of the POLE
and the POLE is the square root of the KILOMETRE
(1,000 METRES), a measure apparently not
established until the late 18th century!

---

* It is interesting to note that there is another measure, the ts'un, equal to one tenth of a ch'ih, i.e. 1.414 inches. 1.414 is the square root of 2.

Sceptics may say that anything can be proved with figures, and doubtless many would wish to echo Anthony Blunt's cry that this is 'mere coincidence . . . an extraordinary coincidence, but a coincidence nevertheless!' Yet, if the kilometre is a scientifically measured and exact proportion of the earth's surface, and the pole is the square root of that measure and the Kung Ch'ih is again the square root of the pole, then I must insist that we should at least consider the possibility that this is not merely coincidence but 'enemy action'.

If indeed we are confronting the 'enemy action' of an extremely sophisticated early culture, then its knowledge and its expertise appear to have been widespread. As the ancient Sumerians, the Chinese, the builders of the Neolithic stone circles and the builders of the cromlech of Rennes-le-Château all seem to have used this system of measure, it is remarkable that the knowledge should have been so completely forgotten. Perhaps, though, it was never entirely forgotten. Although there may be negative evidence for recorded numeracy, Boudet certainly seems to have been aware of something of the sort. Perhaps the knowledge was guarded as privileged information – SOLIS SACERDOTIBUS – 'only for the initiated'.

My excursion along the by-way of historical measure provided fascinating vistas which I had certainly not anticipated. I was forced to remind myself that the starting place for this detour had been the Pentacle of Mountains, and immediately upon bringing this new coincidence of numbers back to Rennes-le-Château, I saw yet another amazing link in the mathematics.

One of the interesting properties of the pentagon is its direct correlation with the Golden Section or Golden Proportion. In simple terms, the Golden Section is the division of a line in the most economical way possible, so that the lesser part is to the greater as the greater is to the whole. Thus, in the diagram below, the line AC is divided at B in such a manner that AB is to BC as BC is to AC. The proportion expressed mathematically is 1:1.618.

A   B   C

The pentagon with its star-pentagram or pentacle, is a Golden Section figure.

In the following diagram, the ratio of the sides (for example AB) and the chords (for example AC) is as 1:1.618. Moreover, the chords intersect each other in the same ratio; for example, AC is cut at F by EB so that AF is to FC as 1 is to 1.618. The same ratio repeats itself

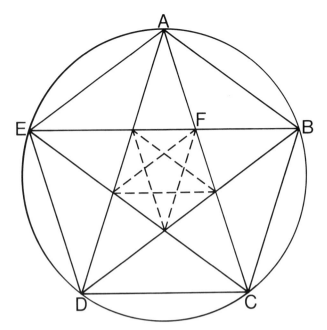

many times within the pentagon. In fact, the ratio can be repeated infinitely by producing further pentagrams within the pentagons created by the intersections of the chords, as indicated by the dotted figure. These figures also diminish in Golden Section progression.

In addition, there is a rectangle which has a very strong and special relationship with a regular pentagon:

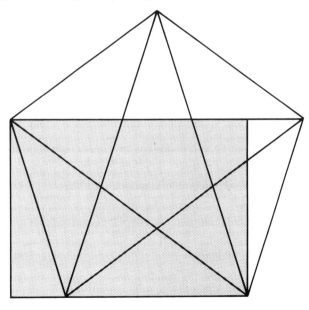

The very precise ratio of height to width in this 'pentagonal' rectangle was used by Poussin for his painting of *The Shepherds of Arcadia*. It is this precisely chosen shape which enabled Professor Cornford to identify the pentagonal geometry. He points out that

> The pentagon, pentagram and embodied Golden Section ratio have enjoyed immense prestige and excited nothing short of reverence among geometers, architects and masons since very ancient times. For the Pythagorean (sixth century BC onwards) the pentagram was a symbol of life, eternity and health: partly I presume by virtue of its Golden Section generating capabilities, and partly because the fifth and final Platonic regular solid, the icosahedron, has twenty pentagonal faces and stood for the universe in Pythagorean cosmogony.

The significant and important numerical relationship embodied in the pentagon, then, is 1 to 1.618. In the matter of the Cromlech Measure, I find coincidence annulled as an explanation by the simple fact that the mile – 63,360 inches – when divided by the pentagonal Golden Section division of 1.618 gives 39,159.456 inches. And the square root of 39,159.456 is 197.88748 which, to little more than a tenth of an inch, is the Pole.

*

I am aware that I have strayed into a dangerous realm. The general scholarly opinion in such matters, quite rightly, fights shy of mathematical proofs which involve minute fractions expressed in a string of decimal places. After all, measures of distance were historically simply a way of defining space in relation to such practical matters as the ownership of land. It would seem, therefore, that early measures had no great need to be anything more than approximate. Even the fiercest of robber barons would hardly don his armour to give battle over an odd foot or two, let alone over divisions of an inch which could not even be seen. All the same, I make no apology for using the convenience of a modern calculator in order to express the measures which I wish to demonstrate. When painfully I attempted the mathematics using paper and pencil, I arrived at figures which showed a discrepancy of less than seven and a half inches over a kilometre – accurate enough for a robber baron and, I hope, for the most sceptical of readers. Even so, my attempt to relate the Rennes-le-Château measure to the English mile falls into that area which a metrological authority has termed 'mathematical romanticism and diffusionism run

88

mad'. But then another expert has told me: 'You cannot argue with the figures.'

Incurable romantic that I am, I cannot resist here inserting a small *jeu d'esprit* engendered by these mathematical games.

Imagine one of Boudet's erudite Celtic Druids, who decides that he wishes to provide a good, usable system of measure for his faithful followers. Accordingly, he measures the earth, takes a quadrant thereof and divides it into inches. (I must here beg the quite serious question of 'whence came the inch?') One 100,000th part of the quadrant is equal to 39,370 inches, of which the square root is 198.41874. Our Druid is only too well aware that his simple and illiterate tribe will not be able to deal with the fractions and so he settles for the round figure of 198, the number of inches in a pole. He multiplies 198 by the Golden Division 1.618, which equals 320.364. Again, for the simple, he rounds off at 320. And thus he gives them the number of poles in a mile.

The Druid divides his new mile unit into inches (who defined the inch?) – and arrives at 63,360. He divides 63,360 by the Golden Division 1.618, which equals 39,159.456. Rounding off as usual gives 39,160 – which is 210 inches less than his quadrant measure of 39,370. And 210 inches make one pole with twelve inches left over to define his new smaller measure, the FOOT!

While this may seem a somewhat flippant way of exploring the mathematics, the mathematics themselves remain serious and, I suggest, merit serious investigation.

*

For the construction of the Holy Place of Rennes-le-Château, the mile and its subdivision, the pole, were the measurements used. It is amusing to consider that our arbitrary mile is not so arbitrary after all. It is 320 times the square root of one 10,000th of a quadrant of the earth's circumference.

In a somewhat obscure Scandinavian publication, *Technikatör-téneti Szemle* (ix. 1977), H. F. Bowsher of Augusta College, Georgia, USA, makes this interesting but unexplained statement: 'The present English units have roots in deep antiquity and have remained virtually unchanged.' Perhaps my interpretation of Boudet's dotty thesis is not a million miles (or one million six hundred thousand kilometres, or three hundred and twenty million poles) from the truth after all.

10

Temple Alignments

The Holy Place which is the subject of this book is the natural pentagon of mountains and the artificial, structured Temple which was built to enclose it. I shall discuss the possible age of the Temple later. For the moment, suffice it to say that the structures which have enabled it to be rediscovered indicate a minimum age of about one thousand years. Unquestionably the expertise existed at the time of the building, both to undertake the construction and to establish the measure, and one must wonder at the incredibly sophisticated culture of its creators. The Temple, I suspect, would never have been rediscovered without the extremely accurate maps which we are only now, in the twentieth century, capable of producing.

I am only too aware that this very sophistication of the builders is exactly the reason why some theorists immediately wish to seek for explanations in Outer Space, or with lost Super-Races. But, as I must again emphasise, there is too long a pathway of investigation to follow before one is left with no other – and more likely – possibility.

First, the Temple itself must be explored. At the moment of writing, I am uncertain of its full extent. My purpose in presenting the evidence which I have assembled so far is to enable readers to embark upon their own voyage of exploration. There may be pathways to follow of which I am not yet aware. The Temple may have recesses which I have not seen and which I may never see, but I hope that others will follow my path into the Holy Place and begin to sense its splendour.

In the pages which follow, I will outline the simple steps which led to the initial discovery and the increasingly complex under-layers which have revealed themselves. This description will enable readers not only to confirm my present findings, but also to extend the work for themselves.

All the evidence which I have so far presented demonstrates with clarity the need to work only with facts which are unarguable. There must be no pursuit of 'possibilities', no drawing of hypothetical conclusions. Each step must be firm and unshakeable, as solid, demonstrable and provable as the Temple itself.

The easiest to find of the elements which define the Temple are the alignments between readily identifiable ancient structures, i.e. churches and castles. I wish to stress that by 'alignments', I do not mean the extremely long-distance lining up of churches or cathedrals over hundreds of miles which some researchers claim to have found and which may, or may not, be the result of chance. Nor do I mean 'ley lines', which seem to be identifiable to dowsers, but have not, to my knowledge, yet been proven to exist in any objectively observable way. Many, if not most, of the alignments which I shall define, cover no more than a few miles and can generally be confirmed by direct line of sight or by sightings from intervening high spots. Moreover, the accurate use, in the placing of structures, of the mile measure and its divisions, as well as the angles of intersecting alignments, will provide the additional proof necessary in order to render the lines meaningful.

So, to begin with, let me state clearly that there is no possibility that the many meaningful alignments of churches and/or castles in the Rennes-le-Château area can be the result of pure chance. One assumes that villages, with their attendant castles and churches, were sited as the result of the haphazard occurrence of, say, a river ford or a defensible hill which might have been chosen for such practical and natural reasons. If, as one might expect, settlement occurred in a thus random fashion, dictated by such considerations, then the aligning of structures would play no part in the intentions of the builders, as it certainly does at Rennes-le-Château.

In order to provide a control – an equivalent area to use for comparison – I suggest that the reader should try the experiment of investigating any map of a similar topography, with open countryside dotted with villages. My own attempts have shown that the placing of three or more castles or churches, in a perfectly straight line over a maximum distance of, say, ten miles, is an extremely rare occurrence.

No more, in fact, than might be expected of coincidence. Rennes-le-Château, however, will present 'enemy action' to a marked, indeed a well-nigh unbelievable degree, and this not only in regard to alignments but also to measured distances.

The initial impetus which led into the discovery was my conviction that David Wood had made a fundamental error in ignoring the original pentagon and failing to incorporate it into his findings. Before his identification of the second pentacle, I saw no reason to suspect that the basic shape might extend beyond the six mountains. Now I could sense that unquestionably it did, even though there was, as yet, no apparent link between the two discoveries. I returned, therefore, to the original pentagon of mountains, to see if it might have any more to show me. For ease of description, I shall henceforth designate the original pentagon as P1 and Wood's pentacle as P2.

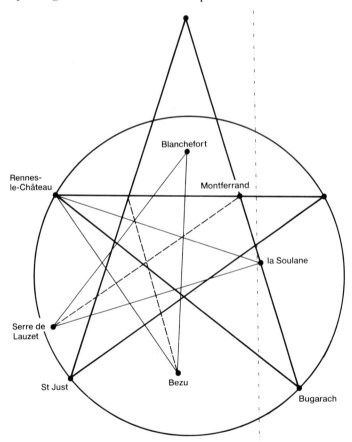

Already Wood had noted that La Pique lay upon one of the alignments of P2. I wondered if there might be other links between the two shapes. Immediately on putting them together, it was evident that the links were there. The most obvious is that both pentacles share Rennes-le-Château as their north-west point. Equally clearly, the eastern-most point of P1 lay exactly on the eastern face of P2. Other and more subtle links were not difficult to find. The castle of Montferrand fixes the north-east angle of P2, and it is precisely placed to bisect the north-east angle of P1. In exactly the same way, the north-west angle of P2 is exactly aligned on the north-west angle of P1.

This elegant bisection of the angles of P1 immediately confirmed the validity of both structures and led me to investigate possible divisions of the remaining angles. Two out of the three immediately produced results.

The church in the village of Le Bezu (not to be confused with the Templar castle of Bezu) lies just outside the pentagonal face of P1 and precisely bisects the Serre de Lauzet/Blanchefort/Bezu angle. The Rennes-le-Château/La Soulane/Serre de Lauzet angle is also bisected, though not by an artificial structure. Another fragment of Rennes-le-Château lore is a legend concerning a shepherd who, pursuing a lost sheep into a cave, supposedly found a treasure. This cave is marked on the map. It is the Aven, a mile and a quarter due south of the village.

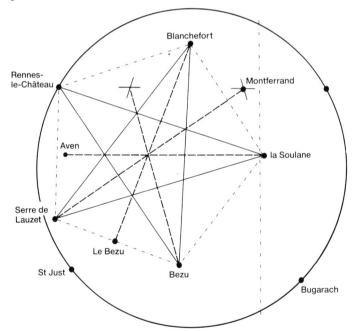

This cavern bisects the fourth angle. There is no obvious bisection of the fifth angle apparent at this stage in the investigation. However, unlike the two upper angles, these two new bisections provided no obvious correlations between the two pentacles. The following diagram shows some other direct, though less obvious, links between the two geometric shapes.

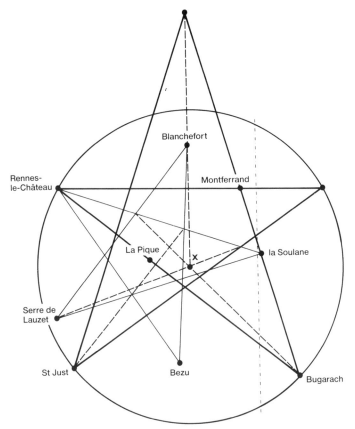

'X' is the centre of the circle.

In addition to the geometric connections, the mile measure and its simple subdivisions became evident. Some of the more significant measures are indicated in the next diagram.

Point 1 to St Just is exactly 7 miles.
Point 2a is at 3½ miles (mid-point).
Point 1 to Point 2 is exactly 3 miles.
Bugarach to Point 4 is exactly 1 mile.
Bugarach to Point 5 is exactly 2 miles.
Bugarach to La Pique is exactly 3½ miles.
Rennes-le-Château to Montferrand is exactly 3½ miles.

94

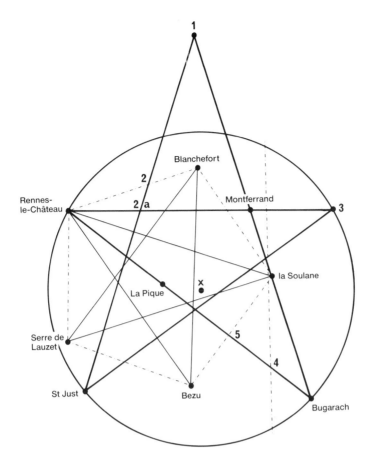

Rennes-le-Château to Bezu is exactly 4 miles.
Rennes-le-Château to La Soulane is exactly 4 miles.

Even the distances *between* the two pentagons show exact measures:

Point 1 to Blanchefort is exactly 2½ miles.
St Just to Bezu is exactly 2 miles.

To insist that such repeated precision of measure is no more than the result of coincidence would be to adopt an attitude of wilful blindness to the clearly visible structuring of this landscape. This newly evident need for careful measure shed fresh light on the extraordinary nature of the first, natural pentagon. It proved to be slightly irregular. This small irregularity leads immediately to the first new discovery outside the area of the two pentacles.

*

The absolutely exact fixing of P1 had been relatively straightforward for three of its five points. Rennes-le-Château had its church; La

95

Soulane and Serre de Lauzet gave exact spot heights. But Bezu Castle had been built atop a long and straggling crest and Blanchefort, as I knew from many visits, had the foundations of more structures upon it than is implied by the one small square indicated on the map. Now, with an awareness of the significance of precise measures, absolute fixes could be made.

The south-eastern end of Bezu's crest, clearly visible as a sighting point from Rennes-le-Château, proved to lie on the exact 4 mile mark. From that point back up to Blanchefort gave the four miles precisely on the castle as indicated on the map, but the distance between the castle as marked and Rennes-le-Château Church proved to be an uncertain measure. Measuring from Rennes-le-Château Castle, however, produced an exact distance of two and a half miles.

In attempting to arrive at an exact fix for Blanchefort, I noticed that David Wood's 'sunrise line' from Rennes-le-Château Church to Arques Church seemed now no longer valid. It was running a good 70 to 80 yards north of Blanchefort Castle. However, I could not discard this 'sunrise line' as a mere inaccuracy, because it was this line which had first drawn attention to the mile measure. (Arques Church was exactly two miles from the Zero Meridian.)

The exact alignment which I had now traced produced a startling new outward movement into the emerging patterns. Rennes-le-Château Church to my fix on Blanchefort did not align with Arques Church. In fact it ran well to the south of Arques village and onwards – to arrive at a grotto. This grotto, clearly marked on the map, is beside the road and exactly six and a half miles from Rennes-le-Château Church! Moreover, this grotto is placed with a beautiful precision in exact relationship not merely with the church at Rennes-le-Château but with the whole of the original pentagon.

The grotto appears to be natural, but such is the incredible exactitude of its placing in relation to the five mountains that a human agency must be suspected. As a purely subjective observation, I note that the cave mouth is intriguingly formed in a shape reminiscent of an arrow-head which points back down the line to Rennes-le-Château.

This new discovery left no further room for doubt concerning the careful and sophisticated structuring of the artificial landscape surrounding the natural pentagon of mountains. But how much more, if anything, remained to be discovered? As a simple first test, to see if more hints of construction would show themselves, I began to search for straightforward alignments between structures and significant

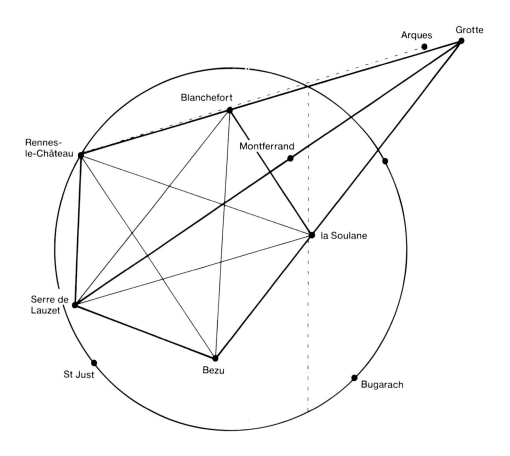

Arques
Grotte
Blanchefort
Rennes-
le-Château
Montferrand
la Soulane
Serre de
Lauzet
St Just
Bezu
Bugarach

The grotto beyond Arques

97

landscape features. As I have already noted, the chance aligning of three or more such points over relatively short distances seems a rare phenomenon. The map immediately confirmed my hunch.

One alignment already identified stood out as being of unusual interest from the large number of significant points which fall upon it. This is the line which forms the eastern face of P2. (Indeed, this has proved to be one of the major controlling lines of the Temple.) It begins at the church in the village of Bugarach and passes through the eastern point of P1 at La Soulane, then through the Castle of Montferrand, the trig point on the Mountain of Cardou, the Castle of Serres and the northern point of P2, which I have designated Combe Loubière, the name of a stream which runs nearby. Bugarach Church also forms another alignment running through La Pique to Rennes-le-Château, both of which figure in the structure of P1. I therefore chose Bugarach Church as the centre in my search for further alignments. Some of the more immediately identifiable lines are shown in the next diagram. A number of the alignments extended over disconcerting distances. Nor could these longer-distance alignments be discounted as coincidence, for the precision of measure could not be ignored. It was soon evident that the Temple covered an extremely large area and the perimeter might not even be confined to the area shown upon my map. I confess that the excitement of this amazing discovery was coloured by the daunting nature of the investigation which was obviously yet to come. Some of the lines which were fixed upon Bugarach Church (e.g. Camps-sur-Agly to Les Sauzils and Montjoi to St Louis) were almost fourteen miles long.

Some of the more easily checked distances are given below. Accepting that even on a large-scale map, exactitude of measure over small distances is impossible, I restrict this list solely to mile and half-mile measures. (On the 1:25,000 scale map, a mile equals 64mm.)

From Bugarach Church to:

St Louis Church	2½ miles	Antugnac Church	8½ miles
La Pique	3½ miles	Missègre Church	9 miles
The Aven	5 miles	Les Sauzils Church	9½ miles
Granès Church	5½ miles	Salza Church	10½ miles
St Julia Church	5½ miles	Montjoi Church	10½ miles
Valmigère Church	7½ miles	Calvaire (north of	
Campagne-les-Bains		Alet)	10½ miles
Church	7½ miles		

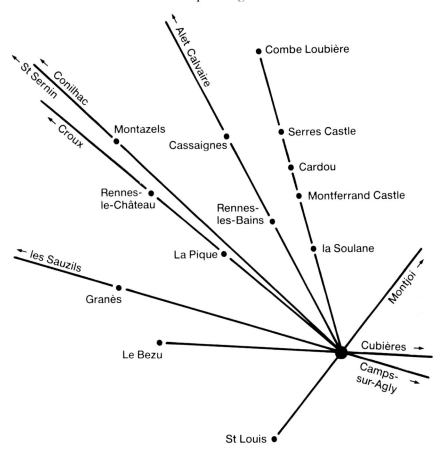

Alignments on Bugarach Church

The Calvaire or wayside cross north of Alet (noted above) completes an alignment through Rennes-les-Bains and Cassaignes. It suggested some new possibilities. Another layer of investigation seemed to lie beyond the major structures in the area. It also offered a fresh consideration for the possible dating of the Temple. Churches and castles figure, of course, in the written records and it is possible to approach a date for their construction. Boudet had insisted that his cromlech was Celtic and older than Christianity. The Alet cross, conforming to both alignment and measured distance, extended the search beyond the placing of churches and castles.

It was immediately apparent that the two megalithic standing stones marked on the map are also linked to the geometry. One of these two stones is quite close to the Poussin Tomb and is marked on the map as Pierre Dressée. The other is five and a half miles north-west on an alignment through the church of St Salvayre.

Christian churches, as is well known, were frequently placed upon earlier holy sites, such as sacred groves or pagan temples. As the investigation began to reveal the extent and complexity of the Temple, it seemed more and more likely that most, if not all, the alignments had originally been marked out by standing stones and so could well, as Boudet had suggested, be relics of much earlier pre-Christian times. Not only churches, but also wayside crosses could mark sites once indicated by standing stones. Indeed, as I began to impose more and more precision upon the alignments I was pursuing, I found frequently that the line would pass well clear of a church, only to end upon a calvaire far from present day habitation.

Combe Loubière, the apex of P2, is a significant example of a fixed point, essential to the geometry of the Temple, but not marked by a church – nor, indeed, by any other structure. Wayside crosses often stand at forks in roads and pathways. The apex of P2, when fixed with precision, proves to be so placed. The two northward-running lines of P2 intersect *exactly* at a road fork on the flank of a hillside. There is nothing at this precise spot, but it is the sort of road junction where one might expect a calvaire to stand. Perhaps once there was a wayside cross here? Or perhaps there was once a standing stone already lost and long forgotten before Christianity set about usurping the old sacred sites. For here, indeed, is the sort of spot which was recognised in pagan belief as being in some way potent. Even in the seventh century, the Church was inveighing against rites still practised at sacred stones, springs, groves and *'places where three trackways meet'*. The essential part played in the geometry by the Combe Loubière road junction suggests that the site must once have been marked. And, as will later become clear, the geometry also leads to seemingly insignificant ruins, to caves and springs scattered about the countryside, all of which are fixed unquestionably by the developing geometric patterns fixed by meaningful distances.

As the search for direct alignments proceeded, it became evident that Bugarach Church was demonstrating a rule rather than an exception. Every church marked upon the map proved to be linked in an extraordinary pattern. This, of course, carries the implication that structures beyond the confines of the present map may prove that the Temple extends even further than my current researches can define. It

The undramatic 'junction of three trackways' at Combe Loubière which is
such an important pivot in the geometry.

is by great good fortune that the major part of the structured Temple
appears to lie on the large-scale map which has been the ground for my
investigation and which covers an area of some 18 miles by 12 miles.
The map itself (IGN Maps numbered 2347 east and 2347 west)
measures almost four feet by two feet nine inches. Within the confines
of my study, it is somewhat difficult to mount, lay out and work upon
the adjoining areas. I have, however, made the attempt. Brief investigation has proved, unsurprisingly, that the alignments continue on
to the adjacent maps though (I must confess, to my relief!) the Temple
appears to grow more diffuse and thinly spread the further it moves
from the natural pentagon of mountains.

While it is my intention to extend the area of my researches, I shall
not pursue that investigation within the context of this book. These
pages are a presentation of my preliminary findings. I leave the wider
study to those of my readers who wish to share the excitement of

discovery. My work will, I hope, serve to indicate the methods to be employed, the clues to follow and the evidence to be sought.

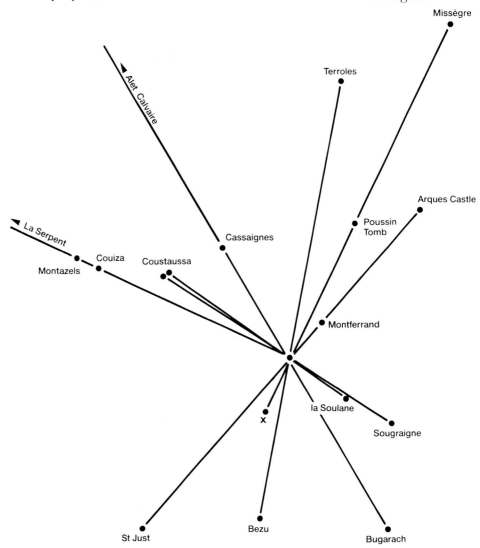

Alignments on Rennes-les-Bains Church

Exact measures from Rennes-les-Bains to:

Serres Church	2	miles	Missègre Church	6½	miles
Poussin Tomb	2½	miles	Cavirac Church	7½	miles
Le Bezu Church	3	miles	Quillan Church	7½	miles
Rennes-le-Château			Roquetaillade Castle	8	miles
(Tour Magdala)	3	miles	Lanet Castle	9½	miles
Granès Church	4	miles			

11

Saunière's Tower

Inevitably, Rennes-le-Château proved to be an extremely important centre for alignments. It also helped with the question of what degree of latitude might be allowed in deciding whether or not an alignment was valid. I had throughout been working on the largest scale map which is available, namely the 1:25,000 scale, in which individual buildings can be clearly differentiated. One millimetre on this map represents 27.5 yards (or 5 poles) on the ground. It is, of course, difficult to measure with accuracy – or even to see clearly – a distance of less than half a millimetre, and I was aware that even the thickness of the line drawn by my pen was covering forty or fifty feet on the ground. None the less it had been suggested to me that a line running merely through a village – and certainly an intersection of lines falling anywhere within a village as marked upon the map – should be considered as satisfactory. This seemed to be allowing far more latitude than was called for by the alignments. Early in my work on the map, I made a note that 'I should allow a tolerance of (say) 1mm to account for opposite ends of a church or castle. This', I wrote, 'is probably over-precise as (e.g.) Arques Castle measures 3 by 2.5mm on the map.'

Allowing only one millimetre of tolerance had shown up the significance of the calvaires which I have already noted above when discussing the alignments on Bugarach Church. I had been rejecting lines which ran more than 1mm (5 poles) away from a structure as marked on the map, even though I was aware that the mere pen-tip was possibly affecting the results. Nevertheless, my self-imposed limitation showed that a line might well pass close to a church without including it, if it was fixed upon a nearby calvaire. It also confirmed that I should not accept an alignment on a structure as valid if it did not fall within these very precise limits.

The map was revealing a truly astounding accuracy of surveying across steep valleys, deep rivers and towering hills. My admiration for the designers was transformed to something like awe in face of their amazing skill. They were not, after all, working as I was, upon a clearly drawn map. Moreover, the distances which they were fixing with such utter precision were on a horizontal plane. A line might begin in the depths of a thickly forested valley and end miles away and far above upon a rock-strewn mountainside. Yet they were able to mark out their geometry over the horizontal distance with a staggering exactitude. How much time, how much effort, how much organisation and skill, how much genius had they employed to construct their incredible Temple? A Temple which was visible only to their gods!

I decided to impose even more stringent limitations and began to draw my lines with an extremely fine pen with a tip of 0.1mm. Theoretically, I could now draw a line which would represent half a pole on the ground – a mere 99 inches. Even allowing for generous error (and failing eyesight), I could now see that some of the Rennes-le-Château alignments fell with exactitude upon either the church or

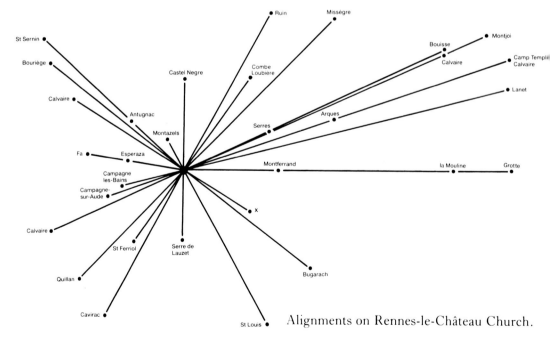

Alignments on Rennes-le-Château Church.

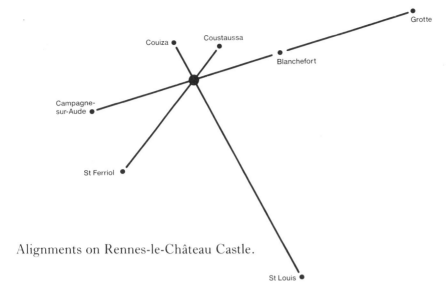

Alignments on Rennes-le-Château Castle.

the château and, to my surprise, an extraordinarily large number – in fact the majority – fell with unerring certainty upon the Tour Magdala, Saunière's library tower. I was forced to accept the evidence that showed the tower had been placed to conform with the alignments. Saunière must have been aware of what I was now slowly and painstakingly rediscovering.

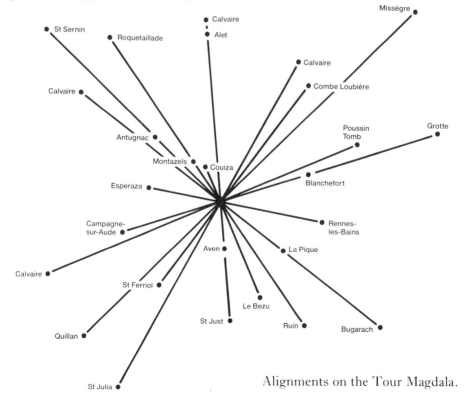

Alignments on the Tour Magdala.

Saunière had built his Tour Magdala as far to the west as was possible within the confines of his hill-top village. The tower is perched in fact on and well-nigh over the sheer drop of the escarpment.

Again, one of the curious anecdotes which are scattered along the trail of the mystery acquired a possible new significance. Saunière apparently had plans for another and much more grandiose tower and in the days just before his death in 1917, we are told, he signed the contract for the work. His new library was to soar to the astonishing height of 60 metres. In the context of the simple treasure story, this seemed nothing more than a pointless extravagance, a rich man's folly. But now the alignments pointed to another and more significant motive.

The 'sunrise line' from Arques church through Blanchefort to Rennes-le-Château had been the first indication of the mile measure. Yet the line itself was slightly less than an exact six miles; it was some eighty or so yards short. I marked with care the exact six-mile point from Arques Church and found that it fell at a spot on the hillside below the Tour Magdala. The contour lines of the map show that it is between 20 and 30 metres lower than the base of the tower. A new tower built on this site in order to complete the alignment would have to be some 60 metres high in order to sight over the Tour Magdala and back down the line. Had this been Saunière's intention? Such a suggestion is, of course, pure hypothesis and impossible to prove. Though it does, in a curious way, tie in with another tale of the priest's doings. In the early days after his initial discovery, we are told that he took to wandering the hillsides. He seems to have claimed that he was collecting stones with which to build a grotto in his church garden. (The remains of such a grotto do indeed exist.) I now wonder if this story is not an attempt to explain a rather more significant activity. Could he have been checking the alignments, verifying the angles, exploring the cromlech? This, too, is an unprovable hypothesis and affects not at all the discovery we are making. It would be satisfying to know that Saunière possessed the secret, but the depth of his resounding silence about it would raise yet more questions which also seem likely to remain without satisfactory or definitive answers – and the Temple poses questions enough of its own.

*

With eyes now opened to the structure and to the superb accuracy of the surveying, the alignments become so easy to find that one cannot but wonder why they have never been noticed before. Curiously, the blinding simplicity of the discovery, once revealed, has been adopted as a sort of bizarre ammunition by those with the odd mentality which insists on denigrating any such utterly unexpected findings. I confess to bewilderment when confronted by the mental contortions and wilful blindness of so many of those who are, perhaps, disturbed by something which does not fit their comfortable – and comforting – view of the world. I have been told that, because my findings are now 'obvious', this can only be proof that the phenomenon is in no way unusual. That an examination of ANY map will probably produce much the same results. Such an argument, of course, is easily refuted simply by making the attempt to find such alignments elsewhere. But the argument totally ignores the reasoning that were churches, castles and mountain tops placed in perfect alignment wherever one might choose to look for them then such would be an even more remarkable fact. And is it not more remarkable still that no-one has ever noticed it? In any case, the possibility that I may have been imagining my results or imposing a wished-for pattern is ruled out by the constant confirmation provided by the consistent use of the mile measure. I urge readers to find that confirmation for themselves by seeking out further alignments and other links between structures upon the map. These are merely the simple building blocks of the Temple; other and even more amazing layers wait to be explored.

12

A Third Pentagon

As the ever-widening area of the geometric Temple began to reveal itself, it was easy to forget that the original starting point had been the near-perfection of the pentagonal layout of the six mountains surrounding the Rennes-le-Château valley. A magnificent reminder came when I turned my attention to the apex of P2 on the road junction at Combe Loubière. As I now expected, direct alignments were not difficult to find. St Julia Church through the spot height on the Serre de Lauzet formed an alignment on Combe Loubière and continued northwards through two more Avens before reaching the top of my map. Arques Church through Combe Loubière aligned on Alet Church, but Combe Loubière showed something more than mere alignments.

As I have already noted, the angles associated with a pentagon are 36°, 72° and 108°. Long days of work with the map had begun to accustom my eye to tell-tale indications. The major Bugarach/Combe Loubière line seemed to lie at what might be a pentagonal angle to the church at Castel Nègre, and measurement proved it to be 108°. I checked the angles to other churches. The result was breathtaking: a stunning regularity revealed itself.

As viewed from Combe Loubière, the angle between Castel Nègre and Bugarach is evenly divided. Each division is marked by a church, castle, or other significant structure and each division is separated from the next with perfect pentagonal symmetry.

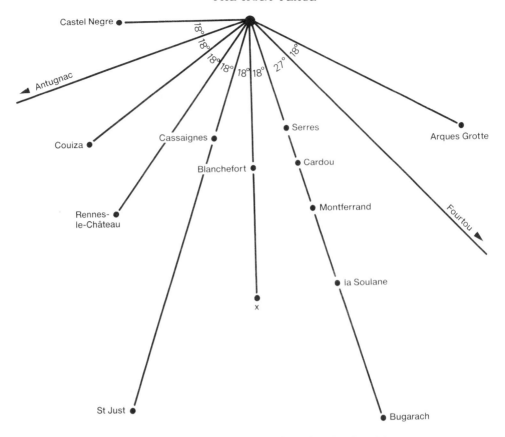

The pentagonal angles based on Combe Loubière

It is a pity that the name 'Pentagon' has been applied to a somewhat more mundane and unimpressive edifice in Washington. The Temple of Rennes-le-Château certainly merits a pentangular appelation, for it is dedicated to the geometry of the Five-Pointed Star with an elegance which is truly superb. The following was one of the first glimpses which I had of a new structural layer based upon that design.

Numerous lines were traced upon my map as I pursued the developing discovery. One or another of these would occasionally lead into a fascinating pattern. This was the case with a line which I had traced from the Church of St Salvayre, a village to the north of the area covered by the map. I had been intrigued to notice that the church in the village of Antugnac is exactly 5 miles from St Salvayre Church and that this alignment, when projected, arrives precisely four miles further on, at the church in the village of Les Sauzils. *Three structures, in perfect alignment over an exact 9 miles!*

A Third Pentagon

With my attention thus drawn to Les Sauzils, I explored from this new point. To my great satisfaction, I found that a line traced from Les Sauzils to the church in the village of Serres aligns precisely upon the Poussin Tomb. Moreover, it arrives there at a distance – again – of 9 miles. From the Poussin Tomb, an alignment through the church in the village of Luc arrives at the church in the village of La Serpent. The measure is an 'imprecise' 8 miles and 40 poles. (40 poles, one furlong, one eighth of a mile.) Even though this line did not repeat the precise 9 mile measure, its contribution to the developing design was immediately confirmed by the map. The church in the village of La Serpent is exactly 5¾ miles from the Aven south of Rennes-le-Château, and this line projected to exactly 9 miles arrives at a Ruin south of the Templar Castle of Bezu. *Again three points, in perfect alignment, over an exact 9 miles.*

This latter point, the Ruin, might be considered coincidental were it not for the fact that it lies 9 miles from the church in the village of St Salvayre, the starting point for this exploration. Another five-pointed star has presented itself.

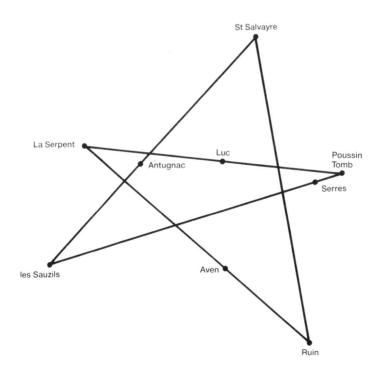

The third pentagon

In the formation of the geometric figure, the ruin south of Bezu is obviously as important as the churches and the tomb which mark the other four points. When, in April 1990, I went to seek out the Bezu Ruin, I was faced with a frustrating disappointment. The hillside proved to be very densely wooded, choked everywhere by matted undergrowth. With visibility hampered in all directions by trees, bramble and scrub, it was impossible to be certain of where exactly on the hillside the ruins – or I – might be. Eventually, I was forced to abandon the search, though not before I had noticed traces of considerable lengths of massive walling showing through the greenery. These walls seemed to be of a sort to support a substantial trackway across the steeply sloping hillside – though this conclusion I arrived at only later, when I had found similar traces at many other of the key points of the geometry. (Later still, at the end of my reconnaissance trip, I was to find even more startling evidence of enormous walling.)

That this fifth point of the new pentacle seems now to be abandoned and ignored suggests that, whatever Poussin, Boudet, Saunière, or anyone else may have known in the past about the cromlech, there may well be aspects which have been completely forgotten. Rediscovery may depend as much upon chance, or the intuition of the researcher, as upon meticulous and painstaking measurements. This new 'irregular' pentagon provides further proof (should more proof be necessary) of the incomparable skill of the builders. Their control of measure, distance and alignment is total, and the complexity of the overall geometric design highlights the brilliance of their surveying techniques. Some of the structural details of the new figure (P3) are indicated in the next diagram.

1. The Bezu Ruin to Point A is exactly 7 miles.
   (This alignment passes through Rennes-le-Château Castle.)
2. Les Sauzils to Point B is exactly 7 miles.
   (This alignment continues on for ¾ of a mile to reach a Calvaire at 'a place where three ways meet' – then arrives at another Calvaire at a 3-way junction south of Valmigère. At 17½ miles it reaches the Church of Lairière.)
3. La Serpent to Point Z is exactly 4 miles.
   (This line reaches Croux Church at 1½ miles and continues to Sougraigne Church.)
4. St Salvayre to Point Z is exactly 5 miles.
   (This line reaches a 3-way junction Calvaire at St Ferriol.)

5. The Poussin Tomb to Point Z is exactly 4½ miles.
   (This line passes through Serres Castle, a ruined Chapel north of
   Coustaussa and, at 7 miles, reaches a 'Tomb' between Fa and
   Esperaza. Projected eastwards this line also runs through Arques
   Castle and, at exactly 6 miles from the Poussin Tomb, reaches a
   Chapel outside the hamlet of St Pancrasse.)

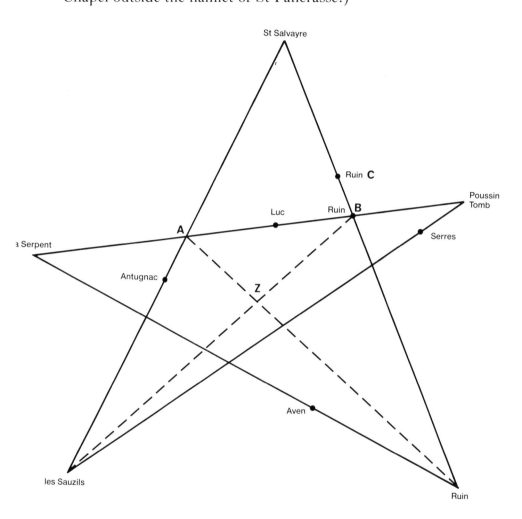

Not to be ignored, of course, are the ruins which mark the angle
of the Pentagon at Point B. The ruin just to the north at Point C is 3
miles from St Salvayre and 6 miles from the Bezu Ruin. Point Z lies in
the valley below Rennes-le-Château. It is close to where the present
road turns off to climb the mountain to the village. Perhaps a marker
stone once indicated the direction of ascent from the valley? St

St Salvayre is a tiny and very ancient church. The floor is extremely old –
perhaps Roman – as are some worked stones visible in the exterior wall. A
'pathway' seems to be defined in the stones of the flooring which leads from
the doorway to the altar.

Salvayre Church, which fixes the northern tip of P3, has proved to be
another crucial point in the geometry.

This church is the pivot of an astonishing swirl of inter-locking five-
pointed stars. The exploration of these other pentagons must await the
unravelling of further skeins of the developing alignments. At this
stage in the investigation, the additional points which define the new
figures are still invisible. There are more, and simpler, discoveries to
be made before they reveal themselves.

The following diagram indicates some of the more direct links
between the new Pentagon, P3 and Wood's discovery, P2. For the sake
of clarity I have omitted P1.

With P1 added, the network of lines and angles begins to assume a
bewildering but beautifully controlled complexity. The next diagram
shows how the three pentagons are impeccably locked together and to
the Combe Loubière fan of 18° pentagonal angles.

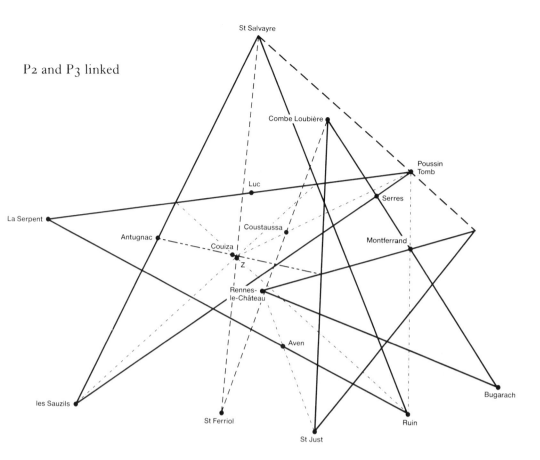

P2 and P3 linked

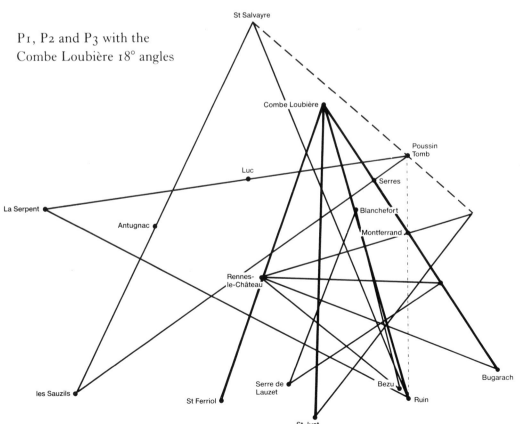

P1, P2 and P3 with the
Combe Loubière 18° angles

As I went deeper and deeper into the structural layers of this marvellous design, I found it necessary to draw back from the map from time to time in order to remind myself that the points which were controlling my drawn lines with such precision were not simply marks on a piece of paper. In the landscape of Rennes-le-Château churches, castles, caves and mountain peaks were displaying in total reality this perfect and level symmetry which was conceived in the mind of a long dead artist/surveyor/engineering genius. The revelation of his master-piece was proving to be as exciting a voyage of discovery as it was possible to imagine. Where would this Master-builder lead me next?

The village of Rennes-le-Château from the air.

13

Enclosing Circles

With the discovery of the second pentacle (P2), David Wood had identified a circle of churches. He had also fixed a second circle of the same size with its centre on the church of Rennes-les-Bains. Superficially, this second circle seemed less interesting than the first, but Wood was able to see his Boat Crescent of Isis and his Ark Crescent of Nut and, satisfied, set off down his own interpretative path.

For my part, I could see only two circles. Their interest for me was the echo which they provided of the two circles incorporated in the parchment geometry. Were there any more such circles? But before I could begin a search, I needed to know the precise size of this circle.

The circle of churches appeared to have a radius of just under three miles. I had already glimpsed a way in which my hypothetical Druid might have arrived at his measures for the foot, the pole and the mile, so where might he go if he needed a larger unit? I made the guess that, in order to keep his system simple, he might choose a neat round figure – say 1,000 poles – three miles plus forty poles, (one furlong – the eighth of a mile). Were there any surviving measures of roughly this length? I wondered about the League. The OED defines the League as 'an itinerary measure of distance . . . usually estimated roughly at about 3 miles.'

The radius of the circle of churches, at just under the perfect measure, was certainly roughly 3 miles, as was the slightly longer hypothetical unit of 1,000 poles. Could either of these be a 'Cromlech League' and, if so, how might it have been derived? If this were to prove the right path to follow, then the logic of the design, I thought, should confirm one or the other.

I contemplated the circle with its overlaid star pattern and noticed that the chord A–B seemed to be of a length which might fit three times within the circumference:

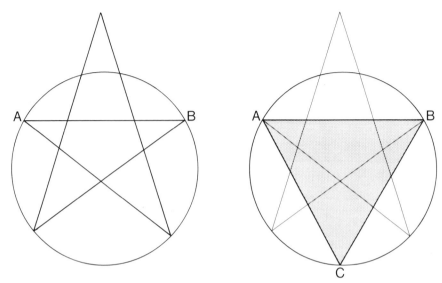

I measured the length of A–B. The line was just over 5 miles long. With care I drew the same line twice more on to the circle and my hunch was confirmed.

A–B = A–C = B–C. Here was an equilateral triangle. (This immediately produces other design implications which must also be left for later investigation.) For the moment, I had a second measure: a chord of roughly 5 miles to put together with the radius of roughly 3 miles. I was thrashing in a geometrical morass, and as I stared at the mountains and valleys drawn upon the map, I remembered the regular pentagon and its Golden Section division 1:1.618. One thousand poles multiplied by the Golden Section Number 1.618 gives 1,618 poles, or 5 miles and 18 poles. This measure is represented on the 1:25,000 scale map by 323.6 millimetres. I measured the chord on my map. The line was between 323 and 324mm long. Here, indeed, was my AB measure of just over five miles. And with this distance fixed, I could now define the radius of the circle.

I learned that, with a chord which fits three times into a circle, the radius of that circle will be equal to .577 times the chord. 1618 × .577 = 933.586 poles. This is 3 miles less 145 yards. And here was the radius of the circle of churches. Just under 3 miles had proved to be

933.586 poles. The map had shown that my two apparently 'rough' measures were with marvellous precision related to my hypothetical – but utterly logical – greater measure of 1,000 poles. My imaginary Druid had demonstrated that he had indeed needed a Cromlech League, and he had shown me how it had been derived and how he had used it.

With the circle radius now logically fixed, I could begin my search for further circles. And I was rewarded with a brilliant new layer of construction.

My eye was becoming educated and I was already learning to identify tell-tale indications. The church in the village of Esperaza seemed to offer promising relationships. It looked a good place to begin the search. Immediately the 933.586 pole length of the circle radius showed itself. Esperaza church was precisely that distance from the churches in the villages of Les Sauzils, St Ferriol, Granès and Coustaussa. Here, then, was another circle. Coustaussa Church had already appeared on the first circle of churches discovered by David Wood. Now it could be seen to be a point of intersection between that original circle and this new one based on Esperaza. Coustaussa therefore seemed to be a logical spot to try as a new centre, and Combe Loubière (the apex of P2) fell satisfyingly into place.

As I tested other circle intersections, a magnificent new demonstration of precision appeared. Churches were not simply aligned. Often the circle radius distance was controlling their placement too.

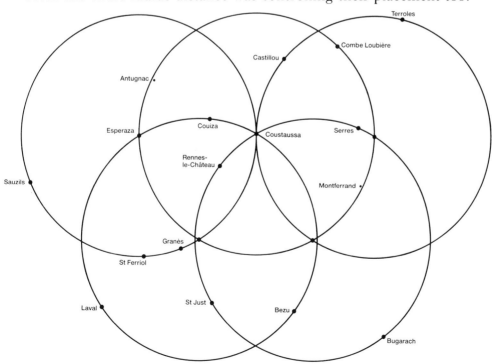

The circles in the previous diagram are by no means all those which can be found. I have chosen for clarity, one particularly simple development in the geometry. More circles overlay this pattern, and of course others will doubtless be revealed when structures on adjacent maps are included.

The circle radius of 933.586 poles is frequently to be found in the distance between structures, some of which are listed below.

Rennes-les-Bains Church	to	Le Bezu Church
Rennes-les-Bains Church	to	Rennes-le-Château Castle
Rennes-les-Bains Church	to	The Aven
Rennes-les-Bains Church	to	Bezu Ruin
Laval Church	to	St Just Church
Auriac Church	to	St Pancrasse Church
Sougraigne Church	to	La Pique
Les Sauzils Church	to	Ginoles Church
Les Sauzils Church	to	St Ferriol Church
Croux Church	to	Bouriège Church
Campagne-sur-Aude Church	to	The Aven
St Julia Church	to	The Aven
Luc Church	to	Serres Church
Veraza Church	to	Poussin Tomb
La Soulane	to	Poussin Tomb
Castillou Church	to	Poussin Tomb
Campagne-sur-Aude Church	to	Rennes-le-Ch. (Tour Magdala)
Calvaire NW of Antugnac	to	Rennes-le-Ch. (Tour Magdala)

The above (far from complete) list already indicates the presence of more circles, but it was the circle on Coustaussa Church which added yet another new dimension to the geometric wonder.

I was puzzled by the fact that Antugnac Church and Montferrand Castle were each slightly inside the Coustaussa circle. The discrepancy was very small – perhaps as little as 10 or 15 poles. All the other structures which were associated with the 933.586 radius circles lay precisely on the line of the circumference and these two did not. I checked their exact distance (five and three quarter miles) and noticed that the line between them ran directly through Coustaussa Church, the centre of the circle. Antugnac and Montferrand were defining a diameter. With this diameter drawn in, I was astonished to see that it lay at an exact 90° to the western face of P2:

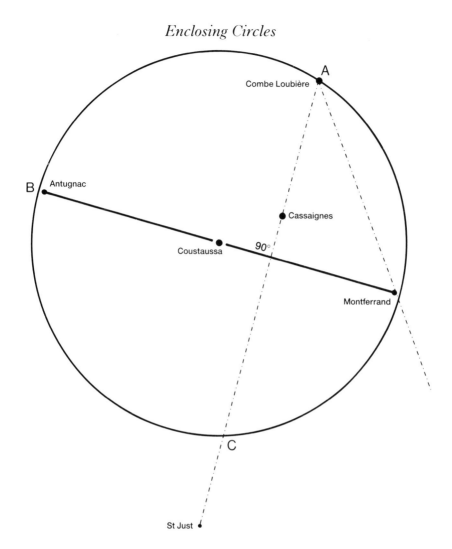

A 90° angle ensures that the distance from Combe Loubière (Point A) to where the diameter cuts the circumference at Antugnac (Point B) is exactly equal to the distance from that point to where the circumference is cut by the western face of P2 (Point C). Again a familiar theme appears. The length of the chord A–B is equal to the radius × 1.618. The western face of P2 is placed with precision in relation to Coustaussa Church, both in angle and distance, to give this magnificent repetition of the Golden Division. Moreover, this ratio of chord to radius produces a beautifully precise pattern. If the chord is repeated around the circle, a ten-pointed star appears – two interlaced pentacles.

We have now moved from the almost regular natural pentagon of mountains, through the curiously distorted pentagons P2 and P3, to this perfect and geometrically controlled figure. Here are the first perfect pentacles marked out in the landscape. The power of these controlling lines seems prodigious in the overall pattern. Almost every line of this complex figure is marked. (See Appendix Two.)

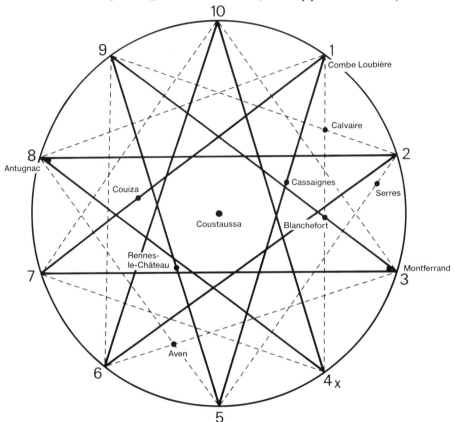

The ten-pointed star is not the first example of regularity in the star-shapes. I showed earlier how the Rennes-le-Château/Montferrand line produced a perfectly regular equilateral triangle, and this is the obvious basis for a hexagram – the six-pointed Star of David, or Seal of Solomon.

To draw in the six-pointed star simply 'because it was there', seemed to be imposing a wished-for result upon the geometry. But the Bugarach/Serres Church line proved to be exactly equal to the Rennes-le-Château/Montferrand line, and so was also hexagonal, though the two lines were not correctly angled to produce the star pattern. Clearly the hexagram had its place in the plan. It was a case of being alert to the possibility and identifying the signal when it appeared. The signal came from Esperaza.

The ruins of Alet Cathedral with the Seal of Solomon visible in the window of Alet Church.

14

Signal from Esperaza

I had already noticed the interesting relationship of the churches which were fixed to the circumference of the circle centred on Esperaza Church, and particularly the distance between the churches of Les Sauzils and St Ferriol. Here, again, was the radius measure of

Esperaza Church – centre of the Seal of Solomon – with Rennes-le-Château dominating the skyline.

933.586 poles. If the Seal of Solomon were to appear in the Esperaza circle, then Les Sauzils and St Ferriol would fix two adjacent points. I drew in the hexagram. Beyond question, I had found the governing shape for the placing of almost every church within the circle.

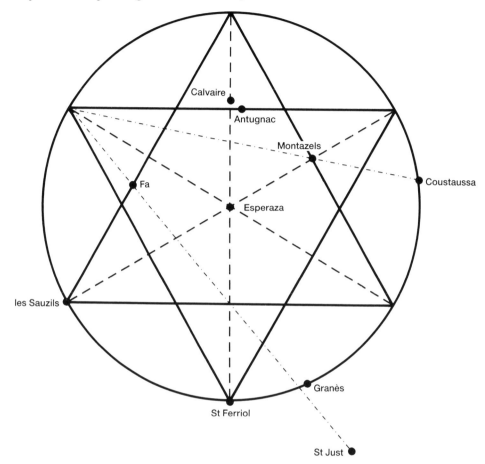

Esperaza and the Seal of Solomon

There are four churches on the circumference of the Esperaza circle and the Seal of Solomon accounts for two of them. I wondered what geometric function I might find for the other two. I was not prepared for the link which they made between the star patterns. Les Sauzils and St Ferriol mark out a chord which fits into the circle six times. Granès and Coustaussa define a longer chord, and their placing was also critical. Here was the joining of the six-pointed star with the five-pointed star, and it was describing a new circle. The centre lay in a place called La Valdieu – the Valley of God.

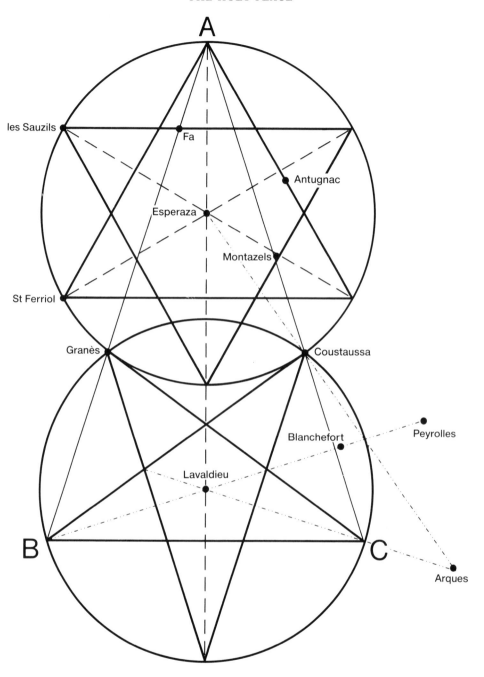

The Seal of Solomon locked into the pentacle centred on La Valdieu.
Distances: A–B = A–C = 7 miles. B–C = 5½ miles.
Coustaussa–Arques = 5 miles

I should point out that there are a number of other ways in which the circle with six-pointed star can be linked with the circle with five-pointed star. One method, which is particularly interesting and which seems to link numerous other structures into the design, is illustrated below.

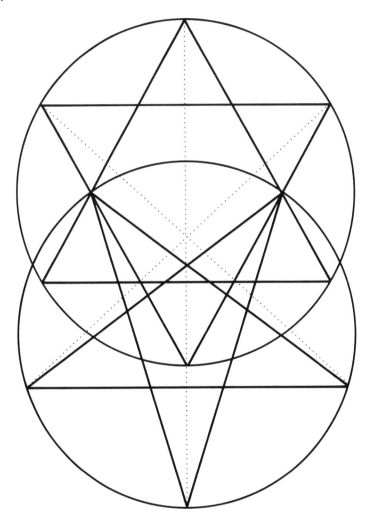

It is worth noting that the correlation of the five- and six-pointed stars seems to be of some interest to students of occult symbolism. Much has been written of the 'secret union' of the two designs. Esperaza's circle of churches certainly exhibits one possibility. Whatever significance may be attached to this fact is too dependent upon subjective interpretation to lie within my brief. I can do no more than observe and record this elegant geometric design.

It would be no exaggeration to say that I was overwhelmed by the beauty and the grandeur of the construction which I found myself exploring. The sheer magnitude of the undertaking was awesome. How much skill, how much labour, how much time had been employed in the accomplishment of this titanic temple? And the result seemed as finely constructed as the intricate mechanism of a watch. No allowance had been made for even the smallest of errors. If one of these churches had been placed even 50 yards from its pre-ordained location then the design would fall apart. Les Sauzils *had* to be a precise distance from St Ferriol. Granès *had* to be fixed with exactitude in relation to Coustaussa. Coustaussa was pinned immaculately to Arques Church and to Esperaza. And so on, and on into a vertiginous maze of controlled complexity. Truly, the building of the Pyramids was a child's game in comparison!

All this great web of design spins out from the six mountains which lie at its heart. Even the great double circle design with pentacle and Seal of Solomon depends for its placing upon the pentagon of natural mountains. Granès Church provides the proof. The design demands that Granès be precisely placed on the Esperaza Circle, and the diagram below clearly shows how rigidly its placing is fixed by the six mountains.

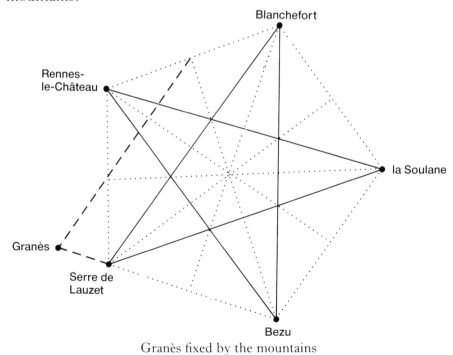

Granès fixed by the mountains

The patterns have now grown so complex that any attempt to draw them all on to one complete design will prove to be self-defeating. The clarity of the inter-relationships of structures becomes swamped by the incredible mass of detail. Could there be a simple basic underlying design?

The circle on Coustaussa Church had shown me many things. Simplest of all had been the 90° angle formed by the Montferrand/Antugnac diameter crossing the western face of P2. The presence of regular geometry – such as the six-pointed star – makes it easy to invent right angles within the designs.

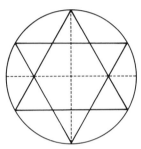

But could I find any simple right-angled intersections which were fixed, not simply by the geometry? Would the alignments of structures provide 90° angles? In other words, could I find a grid? The eastern face of P2 had already shown itself to be an important controlling line, fixing Bugarach, La Soulane, Montferrand, Cardou, Serres Castle and Combe Loubière. I decided to use it as a base line for the next stage of the search. Success was immediate, and impressive.

The village of Laval is almost due west of Bugarach. Laval Church is perfectly aligned with the village churches of Le Bezu, Sougraigne, La Mouline and Auriac. This new line is 90° to the eastern face of P2. Auriac Church is precisely 15 miles from Laval Church. The intersection of the two lines falls neatly 7 miles from Laval and 8 miles from Auriac.

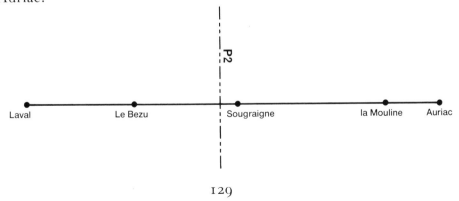

Moreover, placed precisely upon the intersection of these two lines is a spring. I had not noticed this tiny feature when fixing the Bugarach Base Line. It was the first indication that springs, too, should be taken into account in the alignments. Water sources were often sacred to our ancestors. Many of the alignments were to prove to run through them.

As I had hoped, the alignments of churches would produce 90° angles and the existence of the possible grid was confirmed by the fact that the 'sunrise line' through Rennes-le-Château was also at an exact 90° to the eastern face of P2. With the increasing length of the lines, Rennes-le-Château to Arques Church could be seen to be a small part of a much longer alignment. It begins in the west at the church of Campagne-sur-Aude, then passes through the Tour Magdala and the church at Rennes-le-Château, the crest of Blanchefort and the church at Arques – and then continues. At a point 10 miles on from Blanchefort (and at the eastern edge of the map) is a Calvaire in open countryside to the south of the village of Salza. This Calvaire gives a fascinating linking theme to this particular alignment. Campagne-sur-Aude Church is the centre of an ancient Commandery of the Knights Templar. Blanchefort provides a link with the same knightly order: Bertrand de Blanchefort was their fourth Grand Master. The Calvaire south of Salza is located at a place marked upon the map as Camp Templié, the Templar Camp.

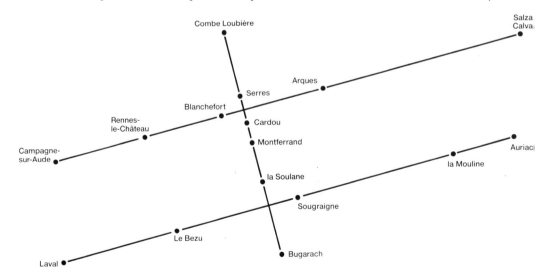

In keeping with the other layers of geometric construction, once the key to the grid has been found, there is no difficulty in discovering further confirming lines.

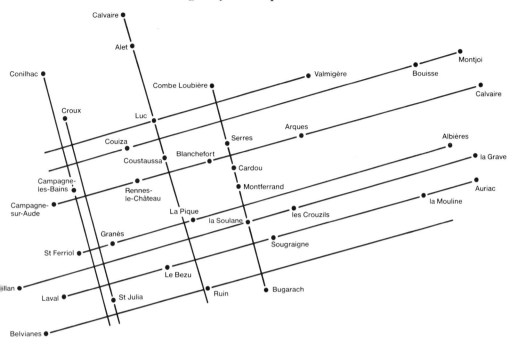

Beginnings of the grid

Although the diagram above is merely an indication of the developing grid lines, it is already clear that the north/south element of the grid seems to be developing to the west of the P2 'Bugarach Base Line'. Controlled unit distances provide the usual confirmation of the validity of the grid lines. Below are noted some of the more immediately identifiable of the measures.

An impressive alignment runs from the Calvaire north of Alet, through Alet Church, Luc Church and Coustaussa Castle. This line runs on to cut the Laval/Auriac line exactly 3 miles from Sougraigne Church.

At an exact one mile to the south of the Laval/Auriac line, another line runs through the Ruin south of Bezu and the church of Belvianes.

The Couiza/Bouisse/Montjoi line is exactly half a mile north of Coustaussa Church. It also runs one mile and one furlong above the 'sunrise line'.

Granès Church is exactly one mile from the Conilhac/Campagne-les-Bains line.

La Pique is a quarter of a mile from the Alet/Coustaussa line.

As already noted, Laval is an exact 7 miles from the Bugarach base line. Couiza divides that distance exactly at three and a half miles.

With a grid now firmly established on the eastern face of P2, it seemed a logical next step to test the western face. Immediately the grid of 90° alignments reappeared.

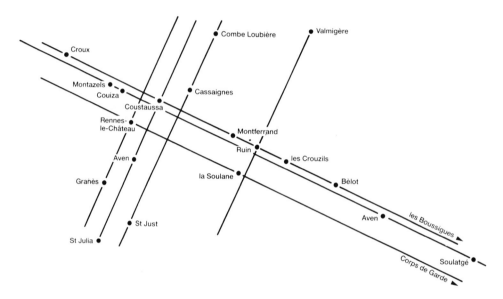

The Croux/Coustaussa/Montferrand line is particularly interesting. It runs on through three sets of ruins. One is unnamed and lies at an exact 2.75 miles from Coustaussa Church. A 90° angle traced northwards from this ruin arrives at Valmigère Church. The other two ruins are marked as Les Crouzils and Belot. They are precisely 2 miles apart. Les Crouzils marks the intersection of this Croux/Montferrand line with the Quillan/La Grave line of the first grid. It is one of the many confirmations that the two grids interlock.

And I must point out that we have not strayed from our original starting point. The grid, though incomplete, is already fixed upon Rennes-le-Château, Blanchefort, La Soulane and La Pique – four of the six mountains which form the Pentagonal Holy Place.

More (and more subtle) alignments contribute to the extending

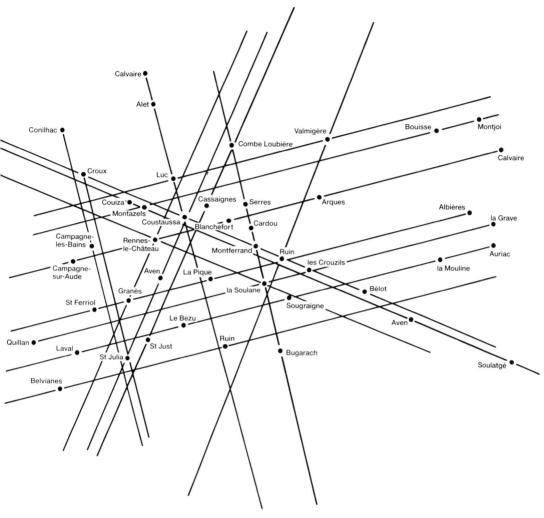

The grids overlaid

network of lines. I have found many but not, I am sure, all that remain to be found. To what overall pattern will the grid conform? Will the distances between lines prove to be rigidly regular? Or related by mathematical progression? Or are they controlled by the Golden Division? Or what?

It is because I cannot answer these questions – because, indeed, I know that there are other questions to be formulated of which I am not even aware – it is for these reasons that I hasten to present this discovery. There is need for a far greater expertise to be brought to bear than I possess in order to reveal the Holy Place in all its majesty.

133

Some of the possessors of that expertise may be obliged to adjust their view of our forebears' talents and skills. Even, it may be, of their acceptance of some of the facts which history teaches.

For me, however, the essential task remains the hunt for the elementary first steps of the construction, the basis of the design – a quest, perhaps fruitless, for the doorway to an easier understanding.

I had set out to find a grid in the hope of identifying a simple underlying pattern. But again I was immersed in a growing maze of alignments. However, by now I had developed a (certainly subjective) feeling that I understood a little of the methods and thinking of the Temple's creator. Although there was an inevitable complexity in his final results, somewhere I should be able to find his simple base. My grid was too complicated.

15

Quest for a Basic Design

Throughout this book I have been retracing the steps of my discovery, fitting together the separate and sometimes unconnected fragments of a gigantic jig-saw whose overall pattern remained a mystery. As I wrote, I was inevitably taken back to the map to verify what I had found in order to describe it with clarity. And as I looked again I found myself confronting new discoveries which increased my understanding of the great design. Now, at this late stage in the recording, I am struggling with some daunting questions. What was the creator of this Temple attempting to do? How did he set about his task? Why does the grid lie where it does? How could the pentagon of mountains have generated all this seeming complexity – and for what purpose?

I am sure that the reader would like definitive answers to such questions, as indeed would I. I can attempt answers, though these would be based on nothing more than guesswork. Some writers on the mystery of Rennes-le-Château are happy to present their theories as solutions, but their subjective solutions have as much validity as mine would have – namely, none.

With the assumption that the reader no longer doubts the reality of the geometry, the alignments and the mathematics, I will now try to follow in a simple and logical fashion the creative steps of the building as they appear to me to have developed. If theoretical answers can be based upon these conclusions, then so much the better. It should be borne in mind, though, that I – and I hope the reader – will hold firmly to the distinction between proven fact and subjective theory.

As I explore the new developments in the discovery, I am aware that, inevitably, some of my earlier conclusions will become slightly modified. I shall, however, leave the 'first thoughts' unamended, as they were necessary steps in the train of deduction.

First, then, came the discovery of the pentagon of mountains, with the unfolding of a basic grid fixed by the placing of that pentagon in the landscape. The first parallel grid lines spring naturally from the geometric shape and the fixed measure provided by the separation of the mountain peaks immediately begins to control the placing of structures.

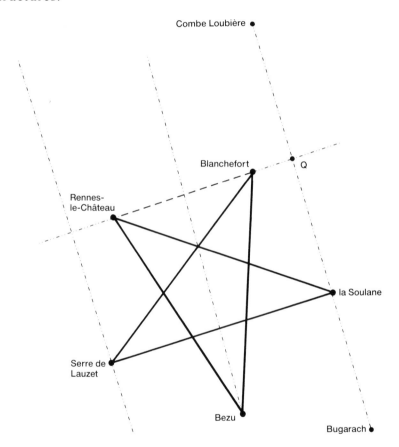

The angle and placing of what I have termed the 'Bugarach Base Line' can now be seen to be rigidly controlled by the geometry of the mountains. That section of the Base Line between La Soulane and Point Q is the side of a rectangle defined by the pentagon, and this precise distance (between La Soulane and Point Q) fixes the positions of both Bugarach and Combe Loubière. That is: Combe Loubière to

Point Q = Point Q to La Soulane = La Soulane to Bugarach. With the first elementary steps thus defined, it is possible to see that the structures, once placed, are all, either simply or subtly, linked to the basic pentagon.

For example, I have already indicated (on p.128) the controlled placing of Granès Church. With the grid in place, Granès helps to define the position of Antugnac:

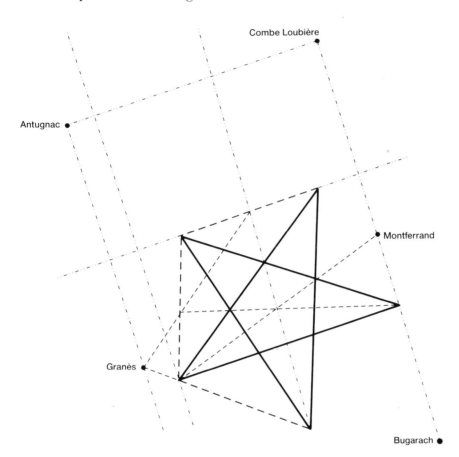

The grid is created by the pentagon. In fact, it should be realised that the pentagonal geometry is all that is necessary for the construction. I have, in a certain sense, imposed the grid upon what is already there in the geometry. The same is true of the circles which I have drawn. Certainly, the simplicity of the circles and the 90° grid help us to see what is there, and together they provide a ripple of logical lines which can now be seen to draw into place church after church, castle after castle, calvaire after calvaire. The simple underlying pattern for which

I had been searching has been obvious from the very beginning. It is the pentagon itself.

Ever more clearly the natural pentagon of mountains can be seen as the basis for the carefully structured design which encloses it. It is the very reason for the existence of the design. My attempts to understand how the designer of the Temple had used his measures seem now to have been distracting from another important question: where did the original measure come from in the first place? Up to this point I had not even begun to approach the possibility that the pentagon of mountains – the god-given holy of holies – might itself have been the prime source. Now that possibility had to be confronted and perhaps one should not be surprised to find that the placing of the mountains seems also to provide the origin for the measure employed in the construction. The distance from Point Q to La Soulane is, as we have seen, fixed by the position of the mountain tops. That distance doubled (e.g. from Point Q to Bugarach, or from La Soulane to Combe Loubière) when divided by the Golden Section proportion of 1.618 is equal to the Circle Radius Measure of 933.586 poles. So the mountains also dictate the measure, and the measure is the English mile and its subdivisions.

This might seem more unlikely to be true than anything so far suggested. How could the mountains have come into existence already neatly and accurately separated by a fixed measure? The question leads to an even more bizarre idea: if the builders of the Temple worked to a fixed measure and the mountains conform to that measure, then did the builders also build the mountains? So wild is the suggestion that it would seem a waste of time even to consider it. But such is the utterly unexpected nature of this whole discovery that I have learned to consider carefully even the most improbable of notions. No longer will I reject anything out of hand. After all, it is not impossible for the mountains to have been 'placed'. Of course the mountains were not created by men, but if the crowning high spots were not exactly where the precision of the design might require, then it is not altogether beyond the bounds of reason to consider an artificial adjustment. An inconveniently placed high spot can be lowered slightly. An artificial high point can be contrived in the necessary place. Such a labour, if reduced to a matter of minor alteration at the very peak of a mountain, is at least possible. I do not suggest that such alterations were actually made, but they certainly may have been.

In the light of such a possibility some complexities, the apparent problems in the design, can now be seen as the direct consequence of slight irregularity in the fixed natural points. The builders are making slight adjustments as they move from irregular to regular geometry. This explains, for instance, why the northern face of the natural pentagon runs on to the Grotto beyond Arques. It is the shift to the 'sunrise line' fixed on Arques Church which provides the regularity necessary for the grid. In a similar way, the southernmost tip of the design at the Templar Castle of Bezu can be seen to mark the base of the natural and irregular design. The adjustment to the grid regularity is achieved by placing the ruin 400 yards to the south.

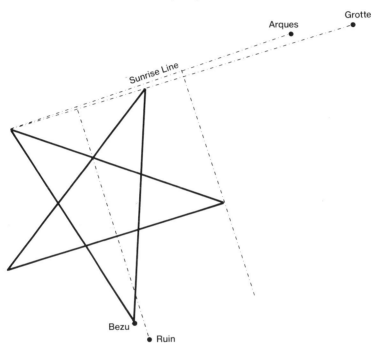

The piecemeal rediscovery of such a complicated yet invisible structure poses a problem not confronted by its builders. The finished masterpiece is in place in all its complexity and the complete design may well be confusing the view of the basic plan. The multiplicity of grid lines which I have been finding may be fogging a simpler picture. In attempting to peer through this fog, I found the following simplified grid which may be closer to the original design. Certainly, the use of the mile measure for fixing the diagonals renders this level of the grid most convincing in its elegance.

Each rectangle is a precise 3 miles across its diagonal, with a pair of rectangles measuring an exact 5 miles. The powerful east/west line fixed by Laval and Auriac provides a perfect 2 mile and one mile division in the rectangle defined by the Bugarach Base Line. Again I must record my admiration for the superlative skill of the builders which was capable of producing such control of measure over extraordinary distances and over such mountainous terrain.

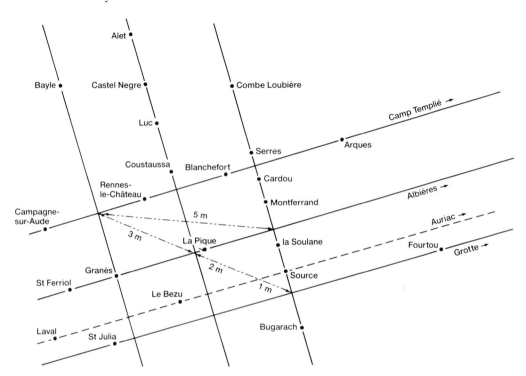

I confess that the geometry is now becoming far too sophisticated for my amateur's grasp. The various skeins of the design are too tangled. As I tease out a strand, I find a new and intricate knot which blocks my progress, and always I am uncomfortably aware that I may be pulling on the wrong thread. I can only struggle towards a sort of understanding which may yet be invalid. Perhaps the simplicity I am seeking lies elsewhere in the recesses of the Temple.

16

Crossing the Paris Meridian

The discovery which I have outlined is already difficult enough to fit into our conventional understanding of the past. What now follows is even more difficult. I shall present proofs of something which, I am told, does not make sense, which I have imagined, which is imposs- ible, or which is merely a coincidence. All these, however, are expressions of opinion. I prefer to rely only upon that which is demonstrable and provable. Let the simple facts speak for themselves.

In 1669, Giovanni Domenico Cassini joined the Académie Royale des Sciences at the invitation of Louis XIV. Two years later, the Paris Observatory was completed and Cassini was appointed its first Direc- tor. In the mid-1680s, he began work on the measurement of the arc of the meridian which runs through Paris. The painstaking labour of measuring the arc between Dunkerque and Perpignan was eventually completed in 1718 by his son, Jacques Cassini, who had succeeded to the Directorship of the Observatory. Although Greenwich was finally adopted as the International Zero Meridian, Cassini's meridian arc is still marked upon French maps as the Paris Zero. It is of interest to us because it runs directly through the Holy Place. It is less than a quarter of a mile from the Poussin Tomb and about 100 yards west of the spot height on La Soulane. Apart from the coincidence of its location, how can this imaginary line, so carefully defined barely three centuries ago, relate to the structure of the Temple of Rennes-le-Château? The idea that they might relate in any way other than coincidentally seems irrational, and yet this investigation will prove beyond any doubt that the Paris Meridian is locked with incredible precision into the geometric layout of the structured landscape around the pentagon of mountains. So elaborate and so detailed are the inter-connections that to argue for coincidence would be like maintaining that a mother's presence at her child's birth is no more than coincidental.

The first indication of the validity of the mile measure came when David Wood noticed that the distance from Arques Church to the Paris Meridian is exactly two miles. I have already made several references to this seemingly irrelevant discovery while refraining from comment or explanation, but now I can approach this most difficult of elements in the mystery against a background of certainty. The diagram below shows the significant links between Wood's P2 and the Paris Meridian.

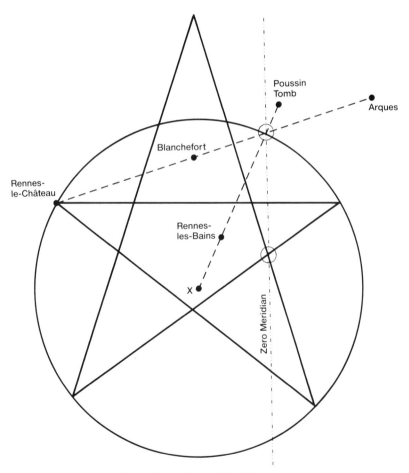

P2 and the Paris Meridian

The 'sunrise line' from Rennes-le-Château to Arques Church cuts the Meridian exactly where it intersects with the line from the Poussin Tomb to Point X, the centre of the first Circle of Churches. The Circle itself also runs through this same point. In addition, the Meridian runs precisely through the angle formed by the two eastern arms of P2. The Paris Meridian and P2 seem to be interacting in some way. More detailed work on the map, however, reveals that the line of the Meridian is inextricably woven into the whole structure of the landscape geometry.

The first hint of this extraordinary fact presented itself during the search for simple alignments. A group intersect with precision upon the Meridian line at a place which I have designated Meridian A (Mer A).

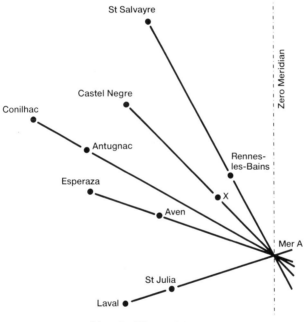

Simple Fix on Mer A

Furthermore, this spot proves to be much more interesting and significant than merely the location of an intersection. It is, for example, exactly one mile from Bugarach Church, 3 miles from Le Bezu Church, 5 miles from Granès Church and 6 miles from St Ferriol Church. Confirmation of the importance of this Meridian Point was evident when it proved to be the base point for yet another St Salvayre pentagon – P4. (See Appendix Three.)

With one point on the Meridian Arc so firmly fixed, there was an inevitable need to investigate the possibility that other alignments might also be related to the Meridian in a similar way. I began to draw in the scores of alignments, projecting to the Meridian those which did not already cross it. To my utter amazement, a pattern began to develop – a pattern which I found almost beyond belief. The alignments were clustering into groups. And those groups were spaced at regular intervals.

For clarity, I have indicated in the next diagram the Meridian divisions as they relate to one church only. Antugnac is particularly well placed to demonstrate the regularity of the spacing. As with the grid, the majority of structures linked to the Meridian divisions lies to the west of the area. Point C is exactly 7 miles from Antugnac Church. Point D, which falls on La Soulane, the eastern tip of P1, is exactly 6½ miles from Antugnac:

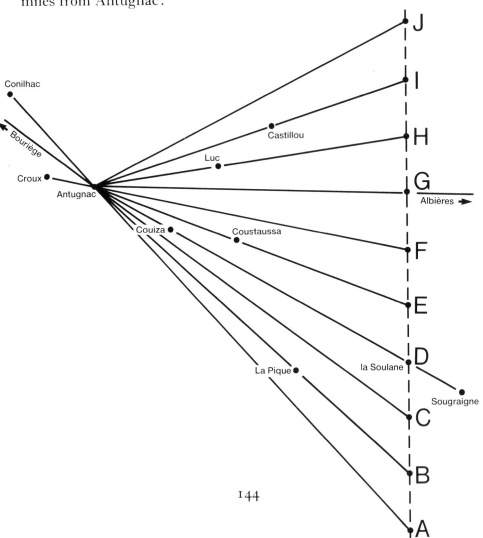

The alignments on the Meridian divisions form a complex network of lines and angles which it is difficult to present clearly in diagrammatic form. It should also be remembered that the ten divisions here illustrated are all that fit into the area covered by my map. Further alignments, and perhaps a clearer structure, may appear when the search is extended. The next diagram, therefore, illustrates only the first level of the developing design:

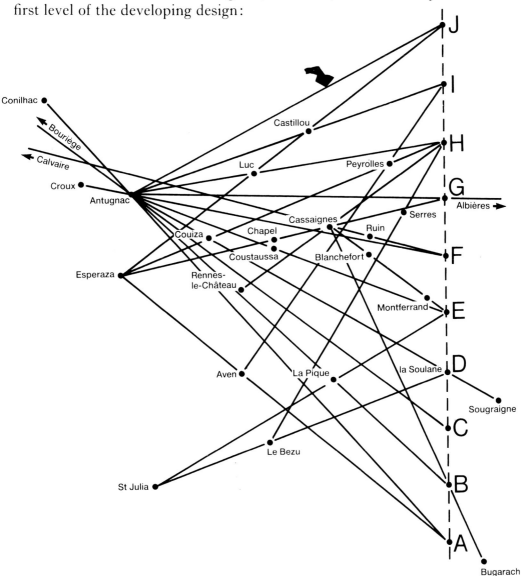

In common with all the other elements in the structure of the Holy Place, fixed measure distances provide constant confirmation of the validity of the alignments. (See Appendix Four.)

There can be no doubt that churches, calvaires, castles and obscure ruins – almost every structure of note upon the map – form an intricate web of alignments which intersect with perfect regularity on the zero meridian. Moreover, that very regularity of spacing carries a familiar indicator of its creator's genius. The distance covered by three of those divisions is the circle radius measure. Each point is separated from the next by exactly one third of 933.586 poles!

*

The indisputable facts set out above present a paradox. How can structures which are demonstrably more than a thousand years old contribute to the definition of an imaginary line conceived centuries after their construction? The answer, of course, is that they cannot – unless the creators of the imaginary line (the Cassinis) were aware of the geometric relationship of the structures. If they were aware of the geometry of Rennes-le-Château why did they not reveal its existence?

The silence of the Cassinis is only a part of this problem. The facts must also be viewed from the reverse angle. The Paris Meridian, which the Cassinis measured and which is still used by the French Geographical Institute, runs exactly along the line of intersections formed by the alignments of structures in the Holy Place. The Paris Meridian is demonstrably the line of intersections. It follows that the line was laid out and fixed by whoever conceived the overall geometric design. But what purpose could this line have served in the remote past? The Meridian Arc is, after all, an accurate marker of longitude – an integral part of modern map-making. Sophisticated, detailed and accurate maps were not produced, presumably, more than a thousand years ago. So, again, what purpose could this line have served?

It is difficult not to be drawn to the obvious conclusion that the Cassini Meridian Line was based upon the 'cromlech intersect division' line. If this is the case, it raises a further disturbing question. The marker point for the Paris Meridian is presently the cross on the Church of the Panthéon in Paris. The line has been slightly adjusted more than once in the past. The fact that modern maps show it now to be an impeccable match with the cromlech division line implies that the adjustments have contributed to that precision. Though in general I find conspiracy theories unacceptable, the problem of the Paris Meridian seems to be indicating some sort of 'enemy action'!

17

The Great Camp

The Temple which I have found at Rennes-le-Château seems to be a completely new and unprecedented discovery. No experts in the matter exist to provide confirmation, guidance or even comment. However, I have shown the results of my research to specialists in some of the various fields upon which my findings have touched. Jim Smith, a lecturer and writer on the history of surveying, having examined the material with great care, said simply: 'You can't argue with facts.' Dr Ian Kinnes, a pre-historian at the British Museum, described the evidence as 'compelling'.

Most interesting was the reaction of a Cambridge lecturer in Pre-History. While unable to dismiss the facts which he could see before him, he was nevertheless constrained to sum up the findings as presenting one of only three alternative explanations.

Namely: 1) 'Outer Space' – which both he and I find nonsensical.

2) 'Conspiracy' – i.e. the map-makers of the French Geographical Institute are continuing (presumably to order) to perpetuate a body of secret knowledge. Again we both agree that this is an extremely unlikely possibility.

3) My methodology is wrong.

This latter is, in his eyes, the most likely, indeed the only possible explanation. He also lays emphasis on the inaccuracy of even the best available maps, which he takes to imply that my results on the map cannot relate to any objective reality on the ground. This line of argument completely begs the question: how does an inaccurate representation come to produce perfect geometry and measure? It also begs another question: what degree of latitude should be allowed in the accuracy of modern maps or the precision of the Rennes-le-Château alignments?*

Christopher Cornford commented: 'Historians have no knowledge of geometry . . . and why should they? But if they were aware of the elegance and coherence of these geometric designs and still believed them to be the result of pure chance – then it would be necessary to accept a coincidence of such astronomical rarity as would, in itself, be an amazing wonder. To ignore evidence of such a compelling nature', he said, 'would be a stain on scholarship.'

The sheer scale of the discovery produces, by its very nature, an unusual problem. There is nothing to see. The magnitude of the Temple renders it invisible. None of the structures which mark out the geometry carry any indication of their part in the gigantic design. Had I discovered the foundations of a lost cathedral or a vanished Stonehenge, then there would be something to touch, to see, to accept. The invisibility of the design requires us to rely upon the measures, the angles, the alignments for any perception of it at all. If careful checks on the ground produce the highly unlikely result that all the geometry, alignments and calculations are based upon error, then another and very tangible mystery remains to be solved.

When I came to visit the area in order to check what I had found on the map, unexpected and visible new evidence came to light. The first steps towards this new discovery had been made in the investigation of the structural details of the Third Pentagon. (See the diagram on p.113.) As I fixed the points of intersection, I noted that Point Y in the diagram below was at an exact 5 miles from the church of La Serpent and 6 miles from the church of Les Sauzils. The measured distances hinted that this new point might merit further study, and indeed it proved to lie upon a very strong alignment.

---

* I have found the maps produced by the IGN to be impressively accurate though small errors can sometimes be detected. An illuminating example was identified during checks prior to publication, when I found an apparent error in one of the alignments. The map on which I was then working was an old one, dating back some twenty years. Verification on the 1982 revision (on which the diagrams in this book are based) showed, however, that the later corrected version conforms precisely with the geometry. This suggests that the very few displacements in the alignments may stem from careless drawing of the map and not from imperfections in the design. Without this unquestionable example, I would never have dared to suggest that the precision of the geometry may sometimes serve to indicate tiny inaccuracies in the map!

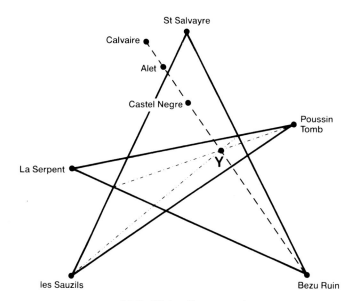

N.B. This alignment is
fixed on Alet Cathedral.
It is distinct from the
Grid Alignment (see p.133)
which runs through Alet Church.

Again fixed distances appeared. From the Calvaire to Alet: 1 mile.
Alet to Castel Nègre: 1½ miles. Castel Nègre to Point Y: 2 miles. A
search for more measured distances quickly produced the following:

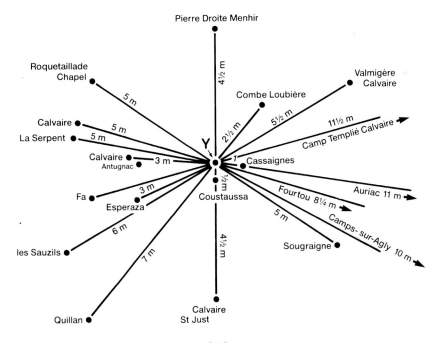

Two virtually intact Capitelles which give a very good idea of their original appearance. These are in such fine condition that it is difficult to assign them a very great age in their present state. Indeed, it has been suggested that such structures were still being erected (or re-erected) as late as the 18th century. Most of the Capitelles on the hillside above Coustaussa show the various stages of centuries of decay.

Massive stone walls at the Great Camp. The mountains in the background are Cardou and Blanchefort.

These walls, higher than a man, stretch for a considerable distance. The gap here visible is not due to the collapse of the stones. Each wall has a 'clean' beginning. The impression given is of a wide 'entrance-way'.

Massive double 'ramparts' at the Great Camp. What form of sheep herding would require such mammoth constructions?

No structure, nor any other feature, is indicated on the map at the intersection Point Y. Beside it, though, is the curious word 'Capitelles', and the surrounding area is marked as 'Camp Grand' – The Great Camp. 'Capitelles', I learned, relates to some dry-stone structures in the area which are considered by the few historians who had made note of them possibly to be shepherds' huts. This, in fact, is the extent of the available information, as no proper archaeological study has ever been made of the area. What little has been written about the early history of this part of France seems to rely on sketchy and often questionable groundwork. From an archaeological point of view, Rennes-le-Château and the surrounding landscape are still virgin and almost completely unexplored territory. The developing details of the structure of the Holy Place, however, suggested that there would be some value in a visit to this 'Great Camp' of 'shepherd's huts'.

The opportunity came in the spring of 1990, when a reconnaissance trip was arranged for a proposed fourth BBC film on Rennes-le-Château. With the director, David Mitchell, I climbed above the village of Coustaussa on a warm April afternoon to examine the Capitelles. We were not prepared for the astonishing sight which we found on the hillside. Not just a few, but hundreds – perhaps thousands – of bee-hive shaped stone structures were scattered across the countryside as far as the eye could see. At first, they were none too easy to see as their colour and the surrounding scrub caused them to merge into the landscape. But the more we looked, the more we found. Some were in remarkably good repair, perhaps built and re-built over centuries. Others were little more than collapsed heaps of stones. Most, however, were clearly and easily identifiable as solid buildings, erected to last, each containing one small room with a doorway and, invariably, a narrow window. Some were square, some rectangular, some circular, some ovoid. Each had a beautifully and skilfully constructed dry-stone domed roof. A very few of the structures seemed to be completely solid, with no interior chamber, which makes it difficult to relate them to the idea of 'shelters'. An historian who has examined my photographs described them as reminiscent of Neolithic bee-hive burial chambers.

If these extraordinary buildings are indeed shepherds' huts, then one is bound to wonder why there should be quite so many of them in this one place. And why do none of them show any sign of ever having contained a hearth or chimney hole to provide warmth for the sheltering shepherd? Then, too, if so many shepherds had gathered in these multitudinous structures, where on earth was the grazing and watering for the huge numbers of sheep which would have accompanied them?

Our brief preliminary visit had raised many questions in our minds. In addition, we had remarked upon traces of very substantial stone walls which we could see criss-crossing the hillside. The areas which these walls enclosed were generally far too small to be marking out fields and the layout seemed wrong if an attempt were made to see them as enclosures for sheep.

David and I decided to return for a second visit with Roy Davies, who was arriving on the following day. Davies had directed two of my Rennes-le-Château films and was now Editor of the BBC's 'Time-watch', successor to the 'Chronicle' series. He has been concerned with the making of films on historical and archaeological subjects for almost two decades. His work has enabled him to visit many ancient sites around the world and his eye can certainly be considered to be educated in such matters. David and I thought it would be interesting to have his response to what we had discovered. And there proved to be yet more to find.

As the three of us climbed higher, pushing our way uncomfortably through dense scrub and bramble, we found ourselves stumbling upon more and yet more substantial stone walls. Some are two metres and more wide, standing to a height of two or three metres. Clearly these are nothing to do with field walls, sheep enclosures, nor any other pastoral activity.

At last we found a great stretch of double wall with traces of buttressing, giving the appearance of nothing so much as defensive ramparts. Roy Davies admitted that of all the archaeological sites he had visited, this was the most reminiscent of Ancient Mycenae in Greece.

The thought that we might be gazing at the remains of a 'Lost City' seemed almost beyond the realm of possibility. Surely there remained no such discoveries still to be made in the last decade of the twentieth century? This question, I would have thought, could only be answered in the affirmative were it not that, a bare three weeks later, on the 20th May 1990, the *Independent on Sunday* reported, under the headline 'Air Survey spots town lost for aeons', the discovery of 'one of the largest prehistoric towns in the British Isles . . . lost for at least 2,000 years'. The world doubtless has yet more forgotten wonders to be revealed!

Roy Davies wondered if this 'city' might not be Reddis/Aereda, the ancient and legendary city of the Visigoths, of which Rennes-le-Château is supposed to be the sole remaining trace.* Certainly, Rennes-le-Château is little more than a mile and a half away and, equally certainly, no other trace of Aereda has so far come to light. However, the Temple alignments which led to the discovery of the 'lost city' suggest something more than we, at this moment, know or understand of the abilities, motivations and activities of the Visigoths. Again we are facing a shadowy past which only skilled archaeological expertise can illumine.

*

As I approach the end of my survey I am conscious that we are rather at the beginning of a long road towards an understanding of what has come to light. Already I am struggling with the huge number of questions which the discovery has raised. The reader, I am sure, will wonder why this book does not explore some of the obvious puzzles which have presented themselves. But most of these were unknown to me when I began to write. Had I known a year ago what I know of the Temple now I would, perhaps, have written a different book. Were I to decide now to write that 'other book', I am sure that twelve months hence I would be presented with the same problem. However, this is not an excuse, but rather an explanation for the lacunae of which I am only too aware.

Apart from the investigation of the 'Great Camp', there are four basic questions which urgently require answers:

1. Who built the Temple?
2. When was it built?
3. How was it built?
4. Why was it built?

To begin reaching for answers, I am bound to move into the dangerous and unsure realm of speculation when I have constantly urged readers to discount anything that is not demonstrable and provable. Yet I can put forward only hypotheses, expressions of my subjective feelings about what I have found. I must therefore emphasise that what follows is *definitely not proven* at this time.

* He decided that the material was nevertheless unsuitable for a film as, in his opinion, it lacked a satisfactory ending: I could not say who had built the Temple – nor why!

18

The Reason Why?

The simple fact that the existence of this wonder has been so thoroughly forgotten, that nothing exists in the historical record which indicates its presence or its purpose, leads one to think that its origins lie in a comparatively distant past. Whatever culture created the Temple was undeniably and amazingly skilled in geometry, mathematics and surveying. Some, and perhaps all of the necessary skills were clearly possessed by the Neolithic communities which produced the Megalithic Stone Circles. The few traces of such communities – standing stones and dolmens – all appear in the alignments. The churches and other structures which now mark out the design could certainly have been placed upon sites which were sacred to the early pagan inhabitants of the area. Even the questionable Boudet seems to consider his cromlech to be Celtic and pre-Christian.

It is my suspicion that the builders of the Temple of Rennes-le-Château will indeed prove to be part of that culture which produced Stonehenge and Carnac, and to date from approximately the same period, i.e. c1500 BC; far enough into the past for their activities to be, if not completely forgotten, then only dim folk memories by the time the Romans came to this part of the world.

It is not necessary to look to Outer Space, nor to Super-Intelligences to account for the evident degree of skill, when one considers the problem of how the surveying and the accuracy were accomplished.

The very elegance and coherence of the geometric design of the Temple has led to a glib assumption that such sophisticated skills were beyond the capabilities of the 'primitive' community which supposedly carried out the work. This assumption is all too easily made by historians and others who find it difficult to accept the reality of the discovery. But, as Professor Cornford has pointed out, such objectors know nothing of geometry . . . and why should they? We seem to be left with two conflicting conclusions. The work was too skilled and could not have been done. It follows that the Temple must be a figment of my imagination – i.e. my methodology is wrong. My opposing stance is simply that, as the Temple's geometry clearly *does* exist, the work must have been within the capabilities of the builders.

I felt bound to confront this problem and to attempt to find out how such apparently complicated mathematics, geometry and construction could have been undertaken without sophisticated measuring and surveying equipment. Could the genius who designed the Temple have issued simple instructions to his labouring force so that they could, for instance, have laid out accurate angles and – (seemingly more complex) – have divided a length into its Golden Section components? Can somebody, with no accurate tools of measurement, multiply a length by 1.618? Without theodolites and other aids, could accurate angles of 36° or 72° or 108° – or even a simple right angle – be reliably defined? The problem seemed a daunting one. The solution, however, proved to be of a delightful simplicity. The 'labourer' needs only to be given some extremely easy instructions.

To lay out a right angle
Take a length of rope and a straight stick. Mark the length of the stick along the rope twelve times. Stretch the rope taut around three pegs so that a triangle is formed with the sides exhibiting 3, 4 and 5 of the divisions. The angle between the side of 3 units and the side of 4 units will be exactly 90°. (There are other and even simpler methods of marking out 90°.)

To produce two lengths in Golden Section relationship
(i.e. in the proportions 1:1.618)
Fold a rope of any length to find its centre. Lay out the rope, marking its two ends and centre with pegs at A-B-C. (See diagram below.) Swing the rope on peg A through an exact 90° (see above). Peg the length again at D. Fix a second rope on peg B and measure the length across the diagonal to peg D. Swing this rope on peg B through peg A and mark with another peg at E.

A-E is in Golden Section relationship to the distance A-C.

To produce a triangle with 'pentagonal' angles (36°-72°-72°)
At C, fix a second rope with length C-E. Swing this rope outwards on C. At the same time swing out A-D on peg A.
Mark where the ends of these two ropes meet at F.
The triangle C-E-F has angles of 36°-72°-72°, (as triangle A-E-F).

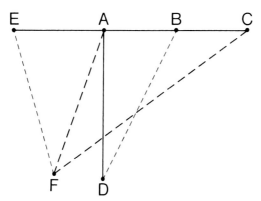

There seems no question that simple techniques and tools would have sufficed if these were employed by people with the requisite organisation and, above all, the time to carry out the work. The demands made upon the societies which built Stonehenge and the stone alignments of Carnac suggest that they would have been equally capable of producing the Rennes-le-Château Temple.

Careful observations of the heavens were undeniably made by the henge builders. Such observations, over sufficient time, would have revealed the pentagonal nature of the movements of Venus, as well as the more easily visible spherical nature of the earth. It is not necessary to assume one vast body of complex knowledge as having sprung full-grown into the consciousness of a 'mystic and enlightened' priesthood. With a gifted 'Pythagoras' to begin a school of study, and with dedicated pupils to carry on the work, the knowledge could have been accumulated over centuries – and centuries would have been required to accomplish the work. There remains the problem of the 'negative evidence for numeracy' and lack of written records that such skills existed and that such expertise was employed. But the Temple, as well as the Megalithic Stone Circles, clearly confirm the existence of the necessary knowledge.

Archaeology will produce answers to the questions 'who?' and 'when?' Current research into early surveying techniques will no doubt provide an indication of 'how?' The question 'why?' will probably never be answered with certainty. We cannot enter into the minds of our remote ancestors. Try as we may, we shall never see the universe as they did, nor fully understand their motives and desires. All the same, my feeling remains that this colossal labour was undertaken as a religious enterprise, a means of enclosing a 'Holy of Holies' (the Pentagon of Mountains) within a coherent Temple. The very size of the Holy Place dictated the gargantuan dimensions of the structure. The fact that the overall shape and size of this Temple remain, for the moment, unclear is partially due to my present inability to find any outer limit to the design. If, indeed, an outer limit was ever defined.

At present, then, the work continues to refine our understanding of the nature of the Temple; to find means of reproducing the precision of the work without recourse to techniques which were not available to the builders; to discover what more may be learned from the remains of the 'Great Camp'. The discovery is too new for many of the questions raised to be answered satisfactorily. Some of the questions may never be resolved. But there is an undeniable excitement to be felt when confronting so unprecedented and unexpected a fragment of our past.

Many professional historians and archaeologists will doubtless react to the evidence by dismissing it out of hand as being so unlikely as to be not worth the investigating. My hope and belief is that such blinkered counsels will not prevail. The weight of evidence cries out for sensible and unbiassed examination.

*

Through the miasma of clues, hints and secret messages which have contributed to this mystery, there have been faint glimpses of an organisation which can best be described as a 'Secret Society'. This is the Priory of Sion to which I have made passing reference in these pages and which was investigated in depth in the two earlier Rennes-le-Château books, *The Holy Blood and the Holy Grail* and *The Messianic Legacy*. Is it possible that this shadowy group may be in possession of part – or perhaps even all – of the details of the Holy Place? There is, of course, no evidence of this. A secret society, after all, does not impart its secrets to the profane (which makes it easy to claim prior knowledge of anything discovered!)

The Priory of Sion has stated that one of its past Grand Masters was the writer and painter Jean Cocteau. Readers may be interested by an example of 'enemy action' which has been identified in his work. (I am grateful to Jim Garretts of the Bury Art Gallery and Museum, Lancs. for drawing my attention to this ingeniously hidden clue.)

Cocteau was one of a number of eminent French artists who were asked to participate in the restoration of the French Church just behind Leicester Square in London, following the extensive damage which it had suffered during the Second World War. His contribution was a fresco for one of the side chapels. In the film *The Shadow of the Templars*, I had drawn attention to the curiosity of the Rose which Cocteau has placed at the foot of the Cross and asked if this 'Rose + Cross' might not be an oblique reference to the Priory of Sion's chosen secondary appellation – 'The Order of the True Rose + Cross'. However, the artist has provided another and more subtle link with the chain of clues which has led to the present discovery. In the *Shepherds of Arcadia*, Poussin has contrived to make the controlling centre of the governing pentacle radiate from the forehead of the Shepherdess. In his fresco, Cocteau has repeated this significant 'conjuring trick'.

He has placed a self-portrait in the left foreground. Behind him are three Roman soldiers each of whom carries a spear. The angles of intersection of these three spears hint at a pentagon whose sides are defined by the distance between the two outer spears along the line of the upper spear. With the pentagon extrapolated from these indications, the centre falls neatly upon the forehead of Cocteau.

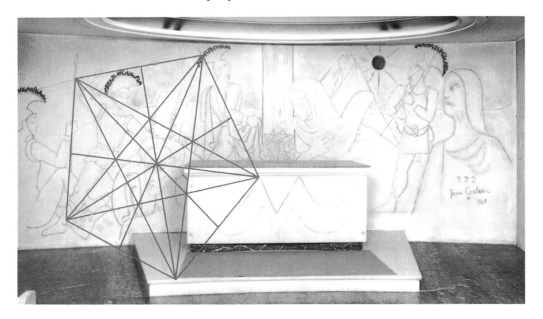

While this may be nothing more than a most extraordinary co-incidence, one is bound to wonder if the Priory of Sion does not have more 'tricks up its sleeve' as well as secrets in its archive.

*

Rennes-le-Château came to the notice of the world because it was the centre of a mystery. Whispers of buried treasure, hints of heresy, suggestions of strange occult rites and of secret societies, even flying saucers have been suggested as the 'truth' behind that mystery. This book does not claim to have solved the riddle. Rather am I aware that I have simply dragged into the light a reason why the centre of all this mystification is Rennes-le-Château and not some other location upon the face of the earth.

And yet still a mystery remains. Over the centuries, countless people must have been aware of the truth of the discovery which I have made. The devisers of the Paris Meridian, the painter Poussin, the priests Bigou, Boudet and Saunière – and how many others? In one way or another they felt the need, like the Barber of Midas, to pass on their secret knowledge, and they did so cryptically. They spoke in riddles because they seemed to be gripped by some mysterious constraint. Why? It is a resonant question, and one which I cannot answer. I certainly feel no such constraint. Nor can I see any reason to conceal such a discovery. It may be, though, that my willingness to reveal it owes less to my knowledge of the discovery than it does to my ignorance of its implications for my predecessors.

I am aware of no necessity to speak in riddles as they have done. But in that necessity may lie the greatest mystery of all.

The Cipher Concealed in Parchment II

Without a full knowledge of the keys and system of encoding, the cipher is unbreakable. It follows therefore that de Sède, (or his informant), who provided the detailed workings, must be in possession of the code-maker's instructions and possibly of the originals of the documents allegedly discovered by Saunière.

Into the text of the Gospel of St John, Chapter XII, verses 1–11, have been inserted 140 extra letters:

```
        V C P S J Q R O
        V Y M Y Y D L T
        P o h R B O X T
        O D J L B K N J
        F Q U E P A J Y
        N P P B F E I E
        L R G H I I R Y
        B T T C V x G D
    A D G E N E S A R E T H
        L U C C V M T E
        J H P N P G S V
        Q J H G M L F T
        S V J L Z Q M T
        O X A N P E M U
        P H K O R P K H
        V J C M C A T L
        V Q X G G N D T
```

In principle, these appear as every seventh letter (there are a few variations). The three letters indicated as lower case in the list above are errors which may, or may not, stem from slips by the original code-maker. I have corrected these three errors in the cipher working below as they have no significant effect on the final message.

It is immediately clear that no computer programme could have been devised which would allow for the arbitrary decisions which need to be made. The first of these decisions is to reject the middle twelve letters (those which spell AD GENESARETH) before the decipherment can even begin.

This leaves two groups of 64 letters. These 128 letters are now to be changed using the key word MORTEPEE by means of a standard and well-known cryptographic system, the Tableau de Vigenère. As can be seen below, the Vigenère system makes use of a table of alphabets, each one shifting progressively down one place from the alphabet preceding.

When de Sède sent the decipherment, he employed a normal 26 letter alphabet and it was this method which was demonstrated in the 'Chronicle' films. I must thank a number of television viewers who wrote to me to point out that the letter W was not commonly incorporated in the French alphabet during the eighteenth century when, it is assumed, the cipher was devised. The removal of the letter W from the table produces a slight simplification in the decipherment process in its latter stages.

THE TABLEAU DE VIGENERE

```
A B C D E F G H I J K L M N O P Q R S T U V X Y Z
B C D E F G H I J K L M N O P Q R S T U V X Y Z A
C D E F G H I J K L M N O P Q R S T U V X Y Z A B
D E F G H I J K L M N O P Q R S T U V X Y Z A B C
E F G H I J K L M N O P Q R S T U V X Y Z A B C D
F G H I J K L M N O P Q R S T U V X Y Z A B C D E
G H I J K L M N O P Q R S T U V X Y Z A B C D E F
H I J K L M N O P Q R S T U V X Y Z A B C D E F G
I J K L M N O P Q R S T U V X Y Z A B C D E F G H
J K L M N O P Q R S T U V X Y Z A B C D E F G H I
K L M N O P Q R S T U V X Y Z A B C D E F G H I J
L M N O P Q R S T U V X Y Z A B C D E F G H I J K
M N O P Q R S T U V X Y Z A B C D E F G H I J K L
N O P Q R S T U V X Y Z A B C D E F G H I J K L M
O P Q R S T U V X Y Z A B C D E F G H I J K L M N
P Q R S T U V X Y Z A B C D E F G H I J K L M N O
Q R S T U V X Y Z A B C D E F G H I J K L M N O P
R S T U V X Y Z A B C D E F G H I J K L M N O P Q
S T U V X Y Z A B C D E F G H I J K L M N O P Q R
T U V X Y Z A B C D E F G H I J K L M N O P Q R S
U V X Y Z A B C D E F G H I J K L M N O P Q R S T
V X Y Z A B C D E F G H I J K L M N O P Q R S T U
X Y Z A B C D E F G H I J K L M N O P Q R S T U V
Y Z A B C D E F G H I J K L M N O P Q R S T U V X
Z A B C D E F G H I J K L M N O P Q R S T U V X Y
```

The coded message is written out with the key word repeated above the letters, thus providing each code letter with its own key letter.

m	o	r	t	e	p	e	e	m	o	r	t	e	p	e	e
V	C	P	S	J	Q	R	O	V	Y	M	Y	Y	D	L	T

m	o	r	t	e	p	e	e	m	o	r	t	e	p	e	e
P	E	F	R	B	O	X	T	O	D	J	L	B	K	N	J

m	o	r	t	e	p	e	e	m	o	r	t	e	p	e	e
F	Q	U	E	P	A	J	Y	N	P	P	B	F	E	I	E

m	o	r	t	e	p	e	e	m	o	r	t	e	p	e	e
L	R	G	H	I	I	R	Y	B	T	T	C	V	T	G	D

m	o	r	t	e	p	e	e	m	o	r	t	e	p	e	e
L	U	C	C	V	M	T	E	J	H	P	N	P	G	S	V

m	o	r	t	e	p	e	e	m	o	r	t	e	p	e	e
Q	J	H	G	M	L	F	T	S	V	J	L	Z	Q	M	T

m	o	r	t	e	p	e	e	m	o	r	t	e	p	e	e
O	X	A	N	P	E	M	U	P	H	K	O	R	P	K	H

m	o	r	t	e	p	e	e	m	o	r	t	e	p	e	e
V	J	C	M	C	A	T	L	V	Q	X	G	G	N	D	T

The first cipher letter 'V' is therefore to be changed by using the key letter which stands above it. This is 'm' – and so the 'm' alphabet is to be used. As is shown in the Tableau de Vigenère above, the letter 'I' falls in the 'V' place in the 'm' alphabet. Consequently, the key letter 'm' changes the code letter 'V' to 'I'. Similarly, the second code letter 'C' is to be changed by means of the 'o' alphabet, which produces the letter 'Q'. And so on . . .

In normal ciphers, this would be sufficient to produce in clear the hidden message. However, in this case, the following (still meaningless) sequence of letters appears:

```
I Q H M N G V S I M E R C S P Y
C S X L F E B Y B R B F F A R N
R F M Y T P N C A E H U J T M I
Y G Y B M Y V C N I L V A J K H
Y J T V A C Y I V V H H T V X A
D Y Z A Q B J Y F K B F D G Q Y
B L R H T T Q Z C V C I V F O L
I Y T G G P Y P I F O A K D H Y
```

Stage Two of the decipherment is to substitute for each letter the one which follows it in the alphabet, so that an 'A' becomes a 'B', a 'B' becomes a 'C', and so on. This simple step produces the following:

```
J  R  I  N  O  H  X  T  J  N  F  S  D  T  Q  Z
D  T  Y  M  G  F  C  Z  C  S  C  G  G  B  S  O
S  G  N  Z  U  Q  O  D  B  F  I  V  K  U  N  J
Z  H  Z  C  N  Z  X  D  O  J  M  X  B  K  L  I
Z  K  U  X  B  D  Z  J  X  X  I  I  U  X  Y  B
E  Z  A  B  R  C  K  Z  G  L  C  G  E  H  R  Z
C  M  S  I  U  U  R  A  D  X  D  J  X  G  P  M
J  Z  U  H  H  Q  Z  Q  J  G  P  B  L  E  I  Z
```

Stage Three is again a Tableau de Vigenère substitution. The key word in this step is no longer MORTEPEE, but is the entire text of the headstone memorial to Marie de Négri:

CTGITNOBLEMARIEDENEGREDARLES
DAMEDHAUPOULDEBLANCHEFORTAGEEDE
SOIXANTESEPTANSDECEDEELEXVII
JANVIERMDCOLXXXIREQUIESCATINPACE

To make up the requisite number of 128 letters, the words PS PRAECUM are added. This new key, moreover, is to be used in reverse! The second key is therefore:

```
M  U  C  E  A  R  P  S  P  E  C  A  P  N  I  T
A  C  S  E  I  U  Q  E  R  I  X  X  X  L  O  C
D  M  R  E  I  V  N  A  J  I  I  V  X  E  L  E
E  D  E  C  E  D  S  N  A  T  P  E  S  E  T  N
A  X  I  O  S  E  D  E  E  G  A  T  R  O  F  E
H  C  N  A  L  B  E  D  L  U  O  P  U  A  H  D
E  M  A  D  S  E  L  R  A  D  E  R  G  E  N  E
D  E  I  R  A  M  E  L  B  O  N  T  I  G  T  C
```

This new key, again used with the Tableau de Vigenère, produces the following sequence:

```
V  M  K  R  O  Z  M  M  Z  R  H  S  S  H  Z  S
D  V  Q  Q  O  A  S  D  T  B  Z  D  D  M  H  Q
V  S  F  D  D  M  C  D  K  N  Q  R  H  Z  Z  N
D  K  D  E  R  C  P  Q  O  D  C  B  T  O  F  V
Z  H  D  L  T  H  C  N  B  D  I  C  M  L  D  F
L  B  N  B  D  D  O  C  R  G  Q  V  Z  H  Z  C
G  Z  S  L  N  Z  D  R  D  A  H  B  D  K  D  Q
M  D  D  Z  H  D  D  C  K  U  D  U  T  K  C  B
```

Stage Four, like Stage Two, is a one-letter shift down the alphabet. (De Sède's original 26 letter alphabet version necessitated a two-letter shift at this stage.) This step produces:

```
X N L S P A N N A S I T T I A T
E X R R P B T E U C A E E N I R
X T G E E N D E L O R S I A A O
E L E F S D Q R P E D C U P G X
A I E M U I D O C E J D N M E G
M C O C E E P D S H R X A I A D
H A T M O A E S E B I C E L E R
N E E A I E E D L V E V U L D C
```

Stage Five divides the 128 letters back into their original two groups of 64. Each group is then laid out in eight rows of eight, as in a chess-board pattern:

8	X	N	L	S	P	A	N	N
7	A	S	I	T	T	I	A	T
6	E	X	R	R	P	B	T	E
5	U	C	A	E	E	N	I	R
4	X	T	G	E	E	N	D	E
3	L	O	R	S	I	A	A	O
2	E	L	E	F	S	D	Q	R
1	P	E	D	C	U	P	G	X
	a	b	c	d	e	f	g	h

A	I	E	M	U	I	D	O	1
C	E	J	D	N	M	E	G	2
M	C	O	C	E	E	P	D	3
S	H	R	X	A	I	A	D	4
H	A	T	M	O	A	E	S	5
E	B	I	C	E	L	E	R	6
N	E	E	A	I	E	E	D	7
L	V	E	V	U	L	D	C	8
a	b	c	d	e	f	g	h	

Stage Six is performed by making a sequence of Chess Knight's moves around the 'board', touching each square only once. This sequence begins on square f6 of the first 'board'. As can be seen above, the vertical square numbering is reversed on the second 'board', thus producing the same pattern, but inverted. The letters are read off in the following sequence:

$f6 - e4 - d6 - c4 - e5 - c6 - d4 - e6 - c5 - d3 - c1 - a2 - b4$
$a6 - b8 - d7 - f8 - h7 - g5 - h3 - f4 - g2 - e1 - c2 - a1 - b3$
$a5 - b7 - d8 - f7 - h8 - g6 - h4 - f5 - e3 - d5 - c3 - e2 - g1$
$f3 - h2 - g4 - h6 - g8 - e7 - c8 - a7 - b5 - a3 - b1 - d2 - f1$
$g3 - h1 - f2 - d1 - b2 - a4 - b6 - a8 - c7 - e8 - g7 - h5$

This operation is the one which finally produces the clear message:

BERGERE PAS DE TENTATION QUE POUSSIN TENIERS
GARDENT LA CLEF PAX DCLXXXI PAR LA CROIX ET CE
CHEVAL DE DIEU J'ACHEVE CE DAEMON DE GARDIEN A
MIDI POMMES BLEUES.

The most surprising – and convincing – proof of the validity of this decipherment and of the bizarre message it contains is the fact that after having changed the letters again and again throughout the process, the sequence has yet reverted exactly to a group of letters visible from the outset. The final message is a perfect anagram of PS PRAECUM plus the entire text of Marie de Négri's headstone.

Alignments of the Ten-pointed Star

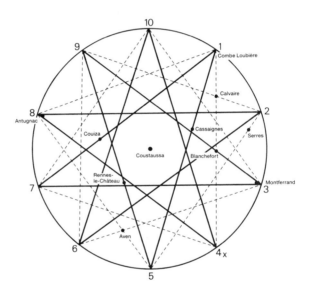

The alignments controlling this design extend beyond the circumference of the circle. In the list below, underlining indicates structures falling within the circumference.

POINTS	FIX LINE THROUGH
1–4	COMBE LOUBIERE – CALVAIRE W OF PEYROLLES – BLANCHEFORT – POINT X (COUME SOURDE) – RUIN S OF BEZU – CALVAIRE W OF ST LOUIS.
4–7	RUIN SE OF POINT X.
7–10	CAMPAGNE-LES-BAINS.
10–3	CALVAIRE N OF ALET – MONTFERRAND.

3–6	<u>AVEN</u>.
6–9	GRANES.
9–2	<u>RUIN AT LA PUJADE</u> – <u>CALVAIRE W OF PEYROLLES</u> – PIERRE DRESSEE.
2–5	<u>SERRES</u> – ST JULIA.
5–8	CALVAIRE S OF ST LOUIS – CALVAIRE N OF LE BEZU – <u>AVEN</u> – ANTUGNAC.
1–5	<u>COMBE LOUBIERE</u> – <u>CASSAIGNES</u> – ST JUST.
5–9	<u>RENNES-LE-CHATEAU (TOUR MAGDALA)</u>.
9–3	<u>BLANCHEFORT</u> – <u>MONTFERRAND</u>.
7–1	CALVAIRE N OF CAMPAGNE-SUR-AUDE – <u>COUIZA</u> – <u>COMBE LOUBIERE</u>.
2–6	ST FERRIOL – CALVAIRE S OF VALMIGERE.
6–10	PIERRE DROITE MENHIR.
10–4	<u>POINT X</u>.
8–2	ARQUES CASTLE – ARQUES GROTTO.

APPENDIX THREE

Fourth Pentagon

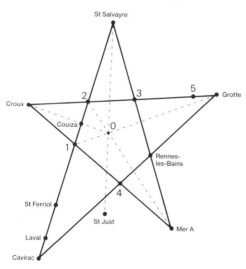

Some of the simpler structural details

CROUX	to	Mer A	9	miles
CROUX	to	GROTTO	9	miles
ST SALVAYRE	to	Mer A	10	miles

| ST SALVAYRE | to | CAVIRAC | 11½ miles |
| CROUX | to | COUIZA | 2 ½ miles |

The distance from the GROTTO to Point 1 is exactly equal to the distance from Mer A to Point 2. The point of intersection (o) lies precisely upon the circumference of the circle centred on ESPERAZA CHURCH.

Exact distances from POINT o

RENNES-LE-CHATEAU			
(TOUR MAGDALA)	1 mile	ANTUGNAC	3 miles
AVEN	2 miles	LE BEZU	3¼ miles
RENNES-LES-BAINS	2½ miles	LA SOULANE	3½ miles
CARDOU	2½ miles	ST JUST*	4 miles
SERRES CHURCH	2½ miles	ST SALVAYRE*	5 miles

* These form a direct alignment of 9 miles.

With so apparently irregular a figure, it is interesting to find numerous internally controlled design elements. For instance: the triangle formed by RENNES-LES-BAINS, Point o and Point 4 is a perfect isosceles, with sides of exact measure – 2½ miles, 2½ miles and 2 miles. CROUX CHURCH forms another perfect isosceles triangle with Points 1 and 2. Point 3 to Point o is exactly 2 miles. And so on. I leave to the reader the further exploration of this fascinating design, with the following suggestion.

A layer of great elegance and complexity in the geometry will be found by projecting the eastern face of P2 northwards to a point exactly 10 miles from BUGARACH CHURCH. The western face of P4 will lock on to this point and produce another beautifully controlled pentagon.

*

P4 presents yet another subject for investigation. Inevitably throughout the research, almost every line drawn has passed through isolated farms, spot heights, anonymous buildings; any one of which may (or may not) be part of the alignments. I have in no case incorporated these into the Temple structure merely because they lay upon a line. This would be to ignore totally the possibility of coincidence and to be straying into the purely subjective choosing of points for no other reason than that they were conveniently placed. (This, indeed, seems to be the method which has contributed to the 'discovery' of the majority of ley-lines.) I have always required something more than a simple alignment before accepting the relevance of any structure. Sometimes this other element has been the location of an important intersection in the geometry. More often it has been the additional coherence of the fixed measures.

In the diagram of P4 above, I have indicated a spot at Point 5 on the line which runs from CROUX to the GROTTO at Arques. This point lies exactly 1 mile from the GROTTO. It is also exactly 5 miles from the church at LA MOULINE, 7 miles from the CALVAIRE at the TEMPLAR CAMP, 8 miles from CROUX and 9 miles from the church at Fa as well as being fixed by numerous other measured distances. The map indicates Point 5 as a small building about 200 yards north-west of ARQUES CASTLE.

As the photograph shows, this building, though falling into ruin, is not particularly old – perhaps about a century – and yet it conforms in many ways to the Temple geometry. This does not necessarily imply that the building was erected to fit the alignments, as seems to have been the case with Saunière's Tour Magdala, though, for lack of evidence, the possibility cannot be discounted. Historians have established great antiquity in the continued use of sites in France and this may be an extraordinary example of such continuity. There is a faint possibility that archaeological investigation may produce evidence for earlier construction here. Or could this be another example of the re-marking of sites in Saunière's time? Whatever may be the explanation for this building, there is no question of its relevance to the geometry.

Distances from the Paris Meridian

The alignments which cross or can be projected on to the Paris Meridian cluster into groups, intersecting the Meridian at regular intervals. Below are listed the EXACT distances of crucial sites in the construction of the Holy Place to the Meridian line at intersection points (labelled A to J) of equal spacing, from south to north:

MER A to

BUGARACH CHURCH	1	mile	ST FERRIOL CHURCH	6	miles
CALVAIRE W OF ST LOUIS	2	miles	ARQUES GROTTO	6½	miles
LE BEZU CHURCH	3	miles	PEYROLLES CHURCH	6½	miles
POINT X	3	miles	ESPERAZA CHURCH	7½	miles
GRANES CHURCH	5	miles	CROUX CHURCH	9	miles
CALVAIRE S OF CAMPS-SUR-AGLY			ST SALVAYRE CHURCH	10	miles
	5	miles	LA SERPENT CHURCH	10½	miles
CHAPEL N OF COUSTAUSSA			SALZA CHURCH	11½	miles
	6	miles	MONTJOI CHURCH	11½	miles

MER B to

BEZU	1½	miles	SOULATGE CHURCH	8½	miles
ST LOUIS CHURCH	2½	miles	ALBIERES CHURCH	8½	miles
LES CROUZILS RUIN	3	miles	ALET CATHEDRAL	9	miles
SERRE DE LAUZET	4	miles	ST SALVAYRE CHURCH	9	miles
RENNES-LE-CHATEAU CHURCH			CALVAIRE N OF LA SERPENT		
	5	miles		10	miles
COUIZA CHURCH	6	miles	ROQUETAILLADE CHURCH		
CUBIERES CHURCH	6½	miles		10½	miles
CAMPAGNE-SUR-AUDE CHURCH					
	7	miles			

MER C to

SOUGRAIGNE CHURCH	1	mile	ANTUGNAC CHURCH	7	miles
POINT X	1½	miles	FA CHURCH	8	miles
LA JACOTTE RUIN	2½	miles	ALBIERES CHURCH	8	miles

CALVAIRE S OF ST LOUIS	3½ miles	LES SAUZILS CHURCH	8½ miles
CASSAIGNES CHURCH	4 miles	CALVAIRE N OF ALET	9 miles
ST JULIA CHURCH	5 miles	LANET CHURCH	9½ miles
ESPERAZA CHURCH	6½ miles		

MER D to

RENNES-LE-CHATEAU CHURCH		BELVIANES CHURCH	8 miles
	4 miles	LANET CHURCH	9 miles
ANTUGNAC CHURCH	6½ miles		

MER E to

RUIN S OF BEZU	3½ miles	AURIAC CHURCH	8 miles
CASTILLOU CHURCH	4 miles	BELVIANES CHURCH	8½ miles
VERAZA CHURCH	4½ miles	ROQUETAILLADE CHURCH	8½ miles
ST JULIA CHURCH	6 miles	CALVAIRE S OF LANET	8½ miles
ALET CHURCH	6½ miles	CALVAIRE NW OF ROQUETAILLADE	
FA CHURCH	7½ miles		10 miles

MER F to

CALVAIRE W OF PEYROLLES		CALVAIRE S OF ST JUST	5½ miles
	2 miles	CALVAIRE NW OF ESPERAZA	
RUIN NE OF COMBE LOUBIERE			6 miles
	3 miles	ST FERRIOL CHURCH	6½ miles
COUSTAUSSA CHURCH	3 miles	CALVAIRE SW OF ALBIERES	
LE BEZU CHURCH	4½ miles		7 miles
CASTEL NEGRE CHURCH	4½ miles	CALVAIRE S OF SOULATGE	9½ miles
MISSEGRE CHURCH	5 miles		

MER G to

CASSAIGNES CHURCH	2 miles	CALVAIRE E OF ST FERRIOL	
TERROLES CHURCH	2½ miles		7 miles
VALMIGERE CHURCH	3 miles	CONILHAC CHURCH	7½ miles
CHAPEL N OF COUSTAUSSA		CALVAIRE S OF LANET	8 miles
	3 miles	MONTJOI CHURCH	8 miles
LUC CHURCH	3½ miles	CAMPS-SUR-AGLY CHURCH	
CASTEL NEGRE CHURCH	4 miles		8 miles
ST SALVAYRE CHURCH	4½ miles	CALVAIRE S OF SALZA	8½ miles
CALVAIRE NW OF MONTAZELS		LAVAL CHURCH	8½ miles
	5 miles	BOURIEGE CHURCH	9 miles
CALVAIRE N OF ALET	6 miles	CALVAIRE NW OF ROQUETAILLADE	
ESPERAZA CHURCH	6 miles		9 miles

MER H to

TERROLES CHURCH	1½ miles	CALVAIRE S OF CAMPS-SUR-AGLY	
CALVAIRE S OF VERAZA	2 miles		9 miles
COUSTAUSSA CASTLE	3½ miles	CUBIERES CHURCH	9½ miles
COUIZA CHURCH	4½ miles	QUILLAN CHURCH	10 miles
SOUGRAIGNE CHURCH	4½ miles	CALVAIRE N OF LASSERRE	
BELOT RUIN	5½ miles		10 miles
CROUX CHURCH	6½ miles	CALVAIRE S OF SOULATGE	
CALVAIRE E OF GRANES	6½ miles		10½ miles
CALVAIRE S OF LANET	8 miles	BELVIANES CHURCH	10½ miles

MER I to

POUSSIN TOMB	2 miles	LE BEZU CHURCH	7 miles
CASSAIGNES CHURCH	3 miles	MONTJOI CHURCH	7½ miles
CARDOU TRIG POINT	3 miles	ST SERNIN CHURCH	9 miles
COUSTAUSSA CHURCH	4 miles	CALVAIRE S OF ST JULIA	9 miles
ROQUETAILLADE CHURCH	7 miles	SOULATGE CHURCH	11 miles
BEZU CASTLE	7 miles	CAVIRAC CHURCH	11 miles

MER J to

ST SALVAYRE CHURCH	2½ miles	AURIAC CHURCH	9 miles
CASTILLOU CHURCH	3 miles	CALVAIRE E OF ST FERRIOL	
COUIZA CHURCH	5½ miles		9 miles
CROUX CHURCH	7 miles	CAMPS-SUR-AGLY CHURCH	
CALVAIRE E OF GRANES	8 miles		10½ miles
BEZU CASTLE	8 miles	CALVAIRE W OF SOULATGE	
CAMPAGNE-SUR-AUDE CHURCH			11½ miles
	8½ miles	BELVIANES CHURCH	12 miles

Investigating the Map

Readers who wish to pursue the research for themselves may find the following practical notes of value.

The best available maps are the 1:25,000 CARTES TOPOGRAPHIQUES published by the Institut Géographique National, 107 rue La Boétie, 75008 Paris. Unfortunately, their large size makes it impossible to reduce them to fit the endpapers of this book. For this reason, the 1:50,000 map has been used in much reduced size. A few sites do not appear marked on this map, but in general it is a useful reference, though unsuitable for tracing out alignments.

The relevant references for the 1:25,000 map are: 2347 ouest QUILLAN for the western half of the area and 2347 est ARQUES for the eastern half. (The Paris Zero Meridian is defined by the join between these two maps.) The maps can be ordered in England from specialist map shops, including Stanfords, 12–14 Long Acre, London WC2.

I suggest that the maps be carefully joined, mounted on an appropriate board and covered by a sheet of clear 2mm plastic. The whole can then be held firmly together with plastic edging trim. If the plastic sheet is carefully wiped over with diluted liquid detergent and allowed to dry, it will be found perfectly possible to draw accurately upon it with pens of the water-soluble type recommended for use with over-head projectors. Errors are then easily removed with a damp sponge.

A useful 'ruler' can be made from a strip of the excess trimmed from the plastic when mounting the map. Marked accurately with division lines every 64mm, the ruler will be scaled to the map in miles. (The smallest practical subdivision is one furlong (one eighth of a mile equals 8mm) which is still clearly visible and measurable).

An equally valuable piece of equipment is a ruler which defines the circle-radius measure and which can act more simply and reliably than a pair of compasses for producing the circles. A scrap of clear plastic roughly nine inches long by one inch should be drilled at one end with a pin-hole. The pin-hole is then placed accurately on, say, Esperaza Church on the map and a hole of sufficient size to take the point of a pen drilled at the exact distance of, say, Les Sauzils Church. This will provide an immutable measure and, with the centre held in place by a mapping-pin through the pin-hole, accurate circles can be traced without the necessity of constantly adjusting compasses to a radius of 186.7mm.

I have also found clear acetate film extremely useful for recording various layers of the geometry, which can then be overlaid, one upon another.

Valuable, too, is a sheet of acetate inscribed with circles of relevant radii. With the centre then placed upon any point, other structures located on 'fixed measures' are immediately visible without the need tediously to measure each point from every other.

I also recommend that churches, castles and other interesting features be highlighted in distinctive colours before mounting the maps. Small details, such as springs and ruins, are easily missed by the tired eye.

Select Bibliography

Michael Baigent, Richard Leigh and Henry Lincoln, *The Holy Blood and the Holy Grail*, Jonathan Cape, London, 1982.

A. E. Berriman, *Historical Metrology*, Dent, London, 1953.

Abbé H. Boudet, *La Vraie Langue Celtique*, Pomiès, Carcassonne, 1886.

Aubrey Burl, *The Stonehenge People*, Dent, London, 1987.

Aubrey Burl, *The Stone Circles of the British Isles*, Yale University Press, 1976.

R. D. Connor, *The Weights & Measures of England*, HMSO Books, Norwich, 1987.

Lucie Lagarde, 'Historique du problème du Méridien origine en France', in *Revue d'Histoire des Sciences*, Paris, 1979.

Richard Morris, *Churches in the Landscape*, Dent, London, 1989.

B. K. Roberts, 'Perspectives on Pre-history', in *An Historical Geography of England & Wales*, ed. R. A. Dodgshon and R. A. Butlin, Academic Press, London, 1978.

Abbé Sabarthès, *Dictionnaire Topographique du Département de l'Aude*, Imprimerie Nationale, Paris, 1912.

G. de Sède, *Le Trésor Maudit*, Editions J'ai Lu, Paris, 1968.

J. R. Smith, *From Plane to Spheroid*, Landmark, California, 1986.

Alexander Thom, 'The Geometry of Megalithic Man,' in *Mathematical Gazette 45*, 1961.

Dom Joseph Vaissete, *Abrégé de l'Histoire Générale de Languedoc*, Paris, 1749.

Tom Williamson and Liz Bellamy, *Ley Lines in Question*, World's Work, 1983.

David Wood, *Genisis*, Baton Press, Tunbridge Wells, 1985.

Acknowledgments

I must express my most grateful thanks to Christopher Cornford, who first suggested the path I should follow; to David Wood, whose work confirmed the validity of my first steps; to Jim Smith, for his unfailing interest and support in ensuring that I never strayed from the objective way; and to Rupert Soskin, for the meticulous care and accuracy with which he has produced the many diagrams so essential for the visualisation of the Holy Place.

I must also thank the villagers of Rennes-le-Château who have, for so long, shown me so much warmth, kindness and friendship.

Picture Credits